DONALD DICKINSON

GREAT MEN OF MICHIGAN
EDITED BY C. WARREN VANDER HILL

DONALD DICKINSON

by

ROBERT BOLT

WILLIAM B. EERDMANS/PUBLISHER

To Carolyn

PREFACE

Donald M. Dickinson is unknown to many Americans. Even within his home state few Michiganians are familiar with this man. He became better known to me after I visited the Michigan Historical Commission Archives in the autumn of 1961 at about the time that Mr. George Wiskemann of Lansing loaned a substantial collection of Dickinson papers to the Archives. Until that time these papers had never been used for historical research. I am grateful to him for giving me the opportunity to examine these papers and thus sparking my interest in Donald Dickinson.

Dickinson is probably unfamiliar to many because so little has been written about him. The most significant publications concerning Dickinson are two short biographical sketches in works of wider scope—one by Arthur Pound in *Michigan and the Cleveland Era* and another by Everett Brown in the *Dictionary of American Biography*. My study of Dickinson led me to believe that he merited more concentration than was given him in these works.

Dickinson was one of the foremost Michigan Democratic leaders during the late nineteenth century. He did much to invigorate the discouraged, downtrodden Democratic party in Michigan during his time. He became a national political figure when Grover Cleveland won the 1884 election, and soon after this victory Cleveland and Dickinson became close associates. In 1887, Cleveland appointed Dickinson postmaster general. As postmaster general, Dickinson adroitly handled the problems that arose when railroad strikes threatened to disrupt the flow of mail in 1888. Despite Cleveland's defeat in 1888, Dickinson continued to work for his nomination and election in 1892. At the 1892 Democratic convention he served as floor leader. After the convention he assumed the chairmanship of the Democratic National Campaign Committee and saw his efforts rewarded with the election of Cleveland. Although Dickinson did not serve in any official capacity during Cleveland's second term, he continued to correspond with and visit the President. It was during his second administration that Cleveland paid Dickinson a high compliment when he wrote, "I wish there were about twenty Dickinsons in the country."

I must acknowledge the labors and contributions of those who in a special way have enabled me to complete this book. I owe much to Dr. Madison Kuhn of Michigan State University, who gave me time, energy, and wise counsel. I also sincerely appreciate the kindness of Dr. Robert Swierenga of Kent State University, who made a number of valuable suggestions after reading the manuscript. Mrs. Geneva Kebler Wiskemann, who had charge of Michigan's archives, went far beyond the call of duty in helping me tell the story of Don Dickinson. My thanks also go to Dr. C. Warren Vander Hill of Ball State University and Mr. Calvin Bulthuis of Wm. B. Eerdmans, whose comments and advice have been useful to me. Finally, I must sincerely recognize the efforts of my wife Carolyn who has spent countless hours typing and reading the manuscript. I express my appreciation for her patient forbearance and assistance.

—Robert Bolt

Grand Rapids, Michigan

CONTENTS

CHAPTER 1

"HERE MY FATHER FOUGHT... HERE WILL I FIGHT"

Donald McDonald Dickinson came into the world on January 17, 1846, on the eve of the most turbulent period that our nation has known. This was the age when Henry Clay proposed compromise in a genuine attempt to avert disunion; when, on the seventh of March, 1850, Daniel Webster rose and forsook all personal ambition in his last great speech defending Clay's proposals even though epithets like "traitor" and "fallen Lucifer" were hurled at him by fellow New Englanders; when "Bully" Brooks caned Charles Sumner in the Senate chamber and then returned to the South to receive miniature canes with inscriptions encouraging Brooks to "Hit him again"; when so many men died in Kansas that the state became known as "bleeding Kansas"; when, in 1858, Abraham Lincoln achieved national prominence by debating with Stephen A. Douglas in hot, dusty Illinois towns; when John Brown became a martyr to the North while horrifying the South; and when Clay's compromise proved to be only a postponement of the inevitable as eleven Southern states seceded from the Union and the war came.

One can surmise from the letters and diaries of Asa C. Dickinson, Donald Dickinson's father, that these and other important events of the day were often topics of discussion and conversation in the Dickinson home. The elder Dickinson was a staunch Democrat and voiced severe criticism of Abraham Lincoln when war was imminent. In a letter written shortly before the outbreak of the Civil War, he charged that only God knew what the policy of Lincoln would be. "I begin to think Old Abe an Old Humbug—without any fixed purpose of his own in particular," he complained. Donald's father foresaw an indecisive Lincoln who could not decide whether the Constitution and the Union or the Republican platform was of greater consequence. Lincoln was "precisely in the predicament of the drunken man who was holding on to the lamp post when accosted by a policeman. 'If I let go,' the inebriate cried, 'I shall fall into the gutter; and if I don't, I shall shed my breeches.' " Like that sot, "poor old Abe actually don't know whether to hold on to the Chicago platform, or whether to let go. He is in a quandary."

9

Even though Lincoln guided the North to victory, Asa Dickinson was certain that the Republicans could not bind up the nation's wounds in the aftermath. The anti-Republican sentiment which pervaded his writings during the Civil War became even more strident after the war when he referred to members of that party as the "Black Republicans." The senior Dickinson denounced Republican reconstruction policy as a blatant attempt "to establish a military despotism in ten states of the American Union. Every man of common sense and common patriotism," he noted, must arouse himself "to the danger that is impending over the length and breadth of our beloved Republic and its once fine institutions." The majority in Congress and the leaders of the Republican party "are traitors to the Constitution and Union and enemies to the form and institutions of our free republican government as founded by our fathers and as administered from the beginning through three-fourths of a century of unprecedented success and prosperity."

The attitudes and words of the father apparently shaped the thinking of his children. For example, a letter from Jerome Dickinson to his father suggests that Jerome thought as his father did. Jerome never evolved into the sophisticate that his younger brother Don became, but he did absorb from his father the notion that simply being a Democrat made a man superior. From the riverboat on which he worked, Jerome wrote:

> The Lieutenant Governor of this state lives here. Is a fine man. Has been in the office several times and talked with me! In operating we have to have a boy to turn a crank which pumps the air. One day we was getting election news and had no boy. He took hold and turned for an hour. So you see he is a Democrat. He asked if my father was not. Said knew he was. Told him was proud to say he was and so was his son.[1]

Two-year-old Donald moved with the Dickinson family from his birthplace along New York's eastern Lake Ontario shore to Michigan in 1848. The new home lay on a small island, named Dickinson Island, in the St. Clair River delta approximately thirty miles north of Detroit. Life on this island was quite pleasant. In later years Dickinson reminisced that as a boy he often took a "licking" from his brother Wane but was always delighted when his sister Martie "made Wane fly like a bumble bee stinger." He first tried riding horseback just after his mother had dressed him for "company." Jack, his horse, pitched young Don over its head "into the soft hog wallow down by the waterfence below the big pear tree," which made him quite unfit to meet the "company." He met a similar fate the first time he tried to milk a cow; she "kicked me head over heels down the hill."

Although life was tranquil on the island, the inaccessibility of their home dictated the Dickinson family's move to Detroit, where Donald began his formal education. The Dickinsons arrived in Detroit about the time that "the yeast of progress began to stir afresh" in that rapidly changing town. So impressed with Detroit's progress was Horace Greeley that, after his first visit to Detroit in 1848, he is reputed to have made his well-known injunction to "go West, young man, go West." There were many signs that indicated Detroit's emergence as an important midwestern city. During the 1840's, distinguished visitors to Detroit included former President Martin Van Buren, Vice President Millard Fillmore, and the noted historian George Bancroft. In 1848, the first Detroit building erected as a theater opened on Jefferson Avenue as the National Theater. Incidentally, in the same year Detroit had the first bathtub installed within its confines. In 1844, park development began with the draining, filling, and raising of the Grand Circus Park area. In 1849, Detroit's citizens felt proud when Jefferson Avenue was paved with cobblestones between Third and Brush Streets. Detroit and Cleveland linked themselves more closely together in 1849 with the establishment of regular steamship service. In 1851, the Detroit Gaslight Company began operation by lighting the main streets of Detroit with coal gas. In the same year that the Dickinsons moved to Detroit, the city was connected with Chicago by rail. Two years later, amid much rejoicing, the first railroad connection between Detroit and New York City became a reality with the extension of the Canadian Great Western Railway to Windsor.[2]

After attending the public schools in Detroit, Dickinson enrolled at the University of Michigan. Like many students away from home, he neglected his family. "I shall have written before and thanked you and Martie for the large and complete assortment of goodies sent in the satchel, but I haven't had any time . . . ." Yet he and his friends enjoyed receiving snacks sent from home. "The raisins and nuts were very nice when my friend came in with a hankerin' or I hankered myself." Dickinson also took pride in his appearance. This characteristic became apparent when he was a university student, for he wrote to his mother that he was much obliged for the extraordinarily immaculate shirt bosoms. "If snow were put by the side of them, it could melt out of shame and confusion at its own audacity in attempting to vie with their whiteness." He found that university life was not all fun. "I am reciting forty pages of tough book law and four lectures per day." For a time Dickinson pursued courses in the Literary Department of the university. He seemed to enjoy creative writing and even composed a poem entitled "The Hills of Washtenaw." Soon, however, the legal profession attracted him, and Dickinson entered the Law Department. He graduated as Bachelor of Laws in March, 1867, and the following May was admitted to practice as attorney and counselor at law.

Even before graduation young Dickinson had developed a keen interest in politics. In a letter to his father prior to the 1864

11

Republican national convention, he predicted that the Republican party would "probably split on A. Lincoln at the coming convention. It looks like it. The name is to be changed again to the 'True Union party.' " On another occasion, in the final stages of political campaigning, Dickinson observed to his mother that he would welcome the honor of putting his shoulder beside his father's, "proving at the polls that the Dickinson clan which pulled so long and so gloriously in victory, so unflinchingly, so unwaveringly in defeat, shall still hew to the will and vigor of Auld Lang Syne grown young again:

Time passes on but . . .
Years ne'er cool the Douglas blood.

No matter how I may waver and grow indifferent in time of peace, no matter how tempted by mincing sophistry and the voice of favor, yet when I hear the sound of blows dealt upon the seamed and sacred frontlets of the brave old guard, my blood will boil! My heart will spring!" With all the enthusiasm and vigor of youth, he vowed to go on fighting for the Democratic party. "Here my Father fought . . . here will I fight. And when Columbia calls the roll, although some names may be missing, yet closing up firmly, when arms are passed down the line, let the answer come strong and brave, and undaunted as of yore—Here! Staunch and true!"

Dickinson's work and growing interest in political affairs did not deter him from serious courtship. On June 15, 1869, he married Frances Platt, daughter of Dr. Alonzo Platt, a prominent Grand Rapids physician. In the years that lay ahead, Fannie, as Dickinson called his wife, aided her husband in achieving a successful political and legal career. For example, Mrs. Dickinson moved very graciously in Washington society when her husband later became one of Grover Cleveland's top aides.

Although Asa Dickinson had sparked his son's initial interest in Democratic politics, Donald's affiliation with the Detroit law firm of Moore and Griffen fanned the flames. The senior partner of the firm, William A. Moore, served as state chairman of the Michigan Democratic party during the Civil War and then as national committeeman from 1868 to 1876. Within a few years Dickinson was to follow in the footsteps of his senior partner.

In 1872, Dickinson grasped the first opportunity to work on an official basis for the Democratic party. Chosen as a delegate from Wayne County, he attended the Democratic state convention which convened on July 2 at Lansing. The main business of the session was to select state delegates to the Democratic national convention. Dickinson won a place on the committee on credentials while William Moore served on the committee on resolutions.

At the Wayne County convention both Moore and Dickinson had supported the candidacy of Horace Greeley as Democratic presidential nominee. Although in the minority at that convention, the

Greeley forces firmly controlled the state convention. Michigan Democrats chose a delegation pledged to support Greeley at the national convention. William A. Moore easily defeated William W. Wheaton in the contest for the first delegate-at-large. This loss caused Wheaton, chairman of the State Central Committee, to resign along with other members of the committee. Foster Pratt of Kalamazoo now became chairman, and Dickinson received his first political appointment when he became secretary of the Democratic State Central Committee. At the Democratic convention in Baltimore, Greeley won the nomination on the first ballot by an overwhelming majority. The party platform left little doubt that corruption in the Grant regime would be one of the main issues of the campaign. One of the major planks called for "thorough reform of the civil service as one of the most pressing necessities of the hour."

Fuel to feed the demand for reform had been furnished in Michigan by a group of Lansing residents who presented a petition to the Michigan House of Representatives requesting an investigation of the conduct of the Commissioner of the State Land Office, Charles A. Edmonds. Edmonds was a Civil War veteran who had lost an arm in that conflict and was named in 1871 to the only important political post he would ever hold. After an exhaustive investigation of the transactions of the land office, the lower house resolved to impeach Edmonds by a vote of seventy-nine to five. Eleven articles of impeachment were presented, charging the commissioner with withholding large tracts of land for the benefit of land dealers and for "private pecuniary consideration to himself" at the expense of genuine settlers, other dealers, and the state. Other articles accused him of such things as buying state land while he was employed by the state, of employing dishonest clerks who sold valuable information contained in the land office, and of drunkenness and adultery. Although the Michigan Senate acquitted Edmonds after hearing the case for four days, the reverberations shook the state and made it evident to some that change was necessary in the administration of the state.[3]

Ill feeling between Republicans and Democrats was not lessened when the issue of reapportionment came up before a special session of the legislature in 1872. Because the Michigan representation in the national House of Representatives had been increased from six to nine, three new Congressional districts were needed. The Republicans seemed intent on gerrymandering to deny any of the new seats to Democrats. One senator denounced the Republican plan by saying, "Let the senator bear in mind one fact at least. At the last election the Democracy of Michigan came within 15,000 votes of the 'great' Republican party, yet it appears to be the main purpose of the legislature to so district the state as to deprive that large minority of the possibility of electing a single representative."

A *Detroit Free Press* editorial similarly charged that the districts were "cut up without any regard to the contiguity of the counties, and without the question of a harmony of interest receiving more than a passing consideration." The Detroit newspaper cited the cases of Macomb, Oakland, Livingston, Washtenaw, Wayne, and Monroe counties. They seemed to be closely bound by "harmonious interests," yet, with the exception of Wayne County, they were placed in districts which usually went heavily Republican, "so that they, as far as Congressional representation from Michigan is concerned, might as well be in the state of Wisconsin."

The Democrats received unexpected support when the well-known Republican Civil War governor, Austin Blair, repudiated the "regular" Republicans and agreed to run for the same office heading both the Democratic and the Liberal Republican state tickets. The national Liberal Republican, or "Mugwump" party had been launched in 1872. Men such as Charles Francis Adams, Lincoln's Ambassador to Great Britain, Carl Schurz, one of the organizers of the Republican party in the 1850's and a long-time supporter of Abraham Lincoln, Whitelaw Reid, assistant editor of the *New York Tribune,* and Charles W. Eliot, the energetic young president of Harvard University, had led the way. This group of Republicans now joined by Blair desired to pacify the South with a more moderate reconstruction policy. They hoped to effect meaningful tariff revisions. Above all, this new organization wished to block the re-election of President Grant and to end the corruption that seemed to pervade all levels of government. In explaining why he could no longer support the Grant administration, Austin Blair said, "I have been in Washington for five years past, and I know that this administration is the most corrupt one this country ever had."

With the state slate chosen and with Election Day slightly more than two months away, the campaign became more heated. Blair campaigned vigorously, declaring that "the Republican party has taken to itself some of the worst rascals in the country, and instead of shaking them from it, cherished them still closer." In September, Governor Horatio Seymour of New York, the unsuccessful Democratic candidate for President in 1868, visited Michigan. In a speech at Utica he declared: "I ask our Republican friends if things have been right in the Federal government. Let us have a man in the Presidential chair who will lay them bare. Then if they are correct you will feel a pride and satisfaction in your party that you can never gain in any other way . . . ." Seymour proposed that nothing be left unexposed and that if "as a result the public mind be aroused, public morality be elevated, and both parties brought to higher standards, I ask you if you as well as we will not be benefited."

Approximately three weeks prior to the election, the Democratic State Executive Committee, of which Dickinson was now secretary, addressed all Democratic and Republican liberals throughout Michigan. In this address the committee reported that during the first half of October elections had been held in six states, and in "four of these states we have been victorious." Liberals in Michigan were strongly urged not "to be idle or indifferent spectators of a political movement so pregnant with important consequences to ourselves." The lengthy statement closed by reaffirming "reform. Then, hopefully, when the sun goes down on the fifth of November, we may return to our friends confident that the virtue and the intelligence of a free people can never be aroused in vain, and that our long distracted country is once more returned to her old paths of purity and peace."

In spite of the sincere optimism that many Democrats felt, various factors vitiated the chance for victory—factors that some Democrats, like enthusiastic young Donald Dickinson, apparently did not deem as important as the election later proved them to be. For example, the fact that the party had nominated Austin Blair for governor was not graciously accepted by all Democrats. Some Democrats could not forget that Blair was a former Republican, and they strongly believed that this "turncoat" should not head their ticket. As far as the presidential nominee was concerned, many Democrats, like Freeman Norvell, editor of the pro-Democratic *Detroit Free Press*, felt that Greeley was not a loyal partisan of their party. When the Democrats nominated Greeley for President, Norvell retired from the editorship which he had held for several years "rather than endorse or advocate the recent attempt at Baltimore to transfer the Democratic party to the support of avowed lifelong enemies of that party, who neither before nor since the nomination have even pretended that they are or ever can be Democrats." Perhaps he recalled that Greeley supposedly had once said, "Not all Democrats are horse thieves, but all horse thieves are Democrats."

This dissatisfaction with Greeley culminated in a "Straight Democratic" convention which met in Louisville, Kentucky early in September, 1872. The convention repudiated Greeley and nominated Charles O'Conor for President. In Michigan the "Straight Democratic" movement climaxed with a convention on September 27 at Jackson. This rump assemblage chose presidential electors, named a state central committee, and nominated a state ticket headed by William M. Ferry of Grand Haven. The person presiding over the convention was none other than William W. Wheaton, former chairman of the Democratic State Central Committee. He declared that a "Straight Democratic" ticket was essential in order to get genuine Democrats to rebuke "the dishonest trickery, which has been attempted to be forced upon the party by false-hearted and weak-minded wirepullers."

15

On the fifth of November, Democratic hopes were dashed when the Republicans won a smashing victory. In Michigan, Grant collected about 60,000 more votes than Greeley and a landslide total of 62.7 per cent of all votes cast for President in the Wolverine State. In the gubernatorial race, the Republican nominee, John J. Bagley, garnered 61.8 per cent of 222,511 votes. Austin Blair received 36.4 per cent, while the minor party candidates captured the remaining votes. Michiganians elected a lone Democrat to the State Senate against thirty-one Republicans, and in the State House of Representatives the Republicans were in the majority by ninety-four to six. All nine Congressional districts sent Republicans to Washington.

Don Dickinson accepted this humiliating defeat bitterly and castigated members of his party for refusing to support the Greeley ticket. The *Free Press* gave some substantiation to Dickinson's conviction. Before the election the Detroit newspaper had hinted that some Democrats might not vote on Election Day because "the leaders of the 'Straight Democratic' movement might urge a stay-at-home policy as a means of concealing the real weakness of the movement." Eight days after the election the *Free Press*, in recapitulating the election results, noted: "But we need go no further than Michigan to find an apt illustration of the fact that a large number of voters abstained from voting and that of this number a great number are opposed to Grant . . . and of the party which supports him." The paper went on to cite some statistics which seemed to support this claim.

On November 29, Horace Greeley died—of a broken heart, Dickinson later wrote. Already disillusioned by the Democratic setback earlier in November, Dickinson now determined to forsake forever the party for which he had labored so diligently during the campaign. On the last day of 1872, he expressed his feelings in a letter to Foster Pratt, chairman of the Democratic State Central Committee. He began by declaring that he had fully made up his mind "never to vote or act with the Democratic party as an organization again." He blamed the Democratic party for Greeley's defeat, affirming that the party "passively or actively, as its members may please to say, defeated Greeley." In so doing, "any link which might still have bound the progressive men of the old organization to it" was broken, Dickinson felt.

Dickinson professed great admiration for Greeley. "Personally," he observed, "I loved him, and not all the slanders and bitter things that were said of him during the campaign swerved me a hair's breadth from my regard for him." Rather than support their candidate, "they have chosen to bicker over the truths told of the ignorance and corruption of other days, by Mr. Greeley, and to revenge the telling of them on their country." Caustically, he ex-

16

pressed more hope in thieves "than of the stolidly ignorant who sway about the feet of truth, crying, 'Crucify him! Crucify him!' "

Dickinson concluded his letter by resigning from the Democratic State Central Committee and promising to "await the new party, which shall take up and carry forward the living principles of our dead leader." At this juncture, it seemed that Donald M. Dickinson's political career had suffered a premature death shortly after its birth.

CHAPTER 2:

"REACHING THE TOPMOST ROUND OF THE LADDER"

The cold, dark winter months that followed the defeat of Horace Greeley seemed to fit the mood of Donald Dickinson. As far as Democratic politics were concerned, he appeared as dormant as the season. His legal practice occupied all of his time and interest. Because of his love for the legal profession, it seemed possible that he might never be active in politics again. Contrasted with Dickinson's political future, the days ahead as a practicing young attorney did indeed appear bright. Richard Dixon, a close friend of the Dickinson family, wrote to Don's mother that her son "is going 'way beyond any of the name.' I rejoice continually the more I see and hear of him, and if he retains his health, he will reach the topmost round of the ladder." A year later Dixon apparently felt that Don had grasped the "topmost round." "I heard a very influential gentleman say to a number of prominent lawyers—his name was Hatch of the firm of Hatch and Cohen—'Don Dickinson of Detroit is the ablest lawyer of his age in this country, and I regard his counsel as valuable as that of any in the city of New York.' "

In spite of this success, Dickinson found the political arena too fascinating to forsake forever. Although he had vowed "never to vote or act with the Democratic party as an organization again," he was persuaded in time by William Moore, his senior law partner and a loyal Democrat, not to follow this course. Thus, by 1874 he was eager to throw himself into the struggle to make the Democratic party more competitive in Michigan. Democratic leaders were quite willing to welcome him back into their ranks; and so, in 1874, Dickinson played an active role in a campaign which saw the Democrats make a rather surprising comeback. As a result of this election, the number of Democratic state senators went from one to fourteen, and in the State House of Representatives the Republicans lost forty-one seats. The Democrats won three out of nine seats in the national House of Representatives.[1] This marked the first time since the Civil War that Michigan had had any Democratic congressmen.

In 1876, Dickinson climbed to the top of the Democratic party organization in Michigan when fellow Democrats named him chairman of the State Central Committee. The state chairman of a major party in Michigan exercised a great deal of political power until the passage of a state-wide direct primary law in 1909. Adoption of the direct primary in Michigan made a potential candidate for governor less dependent on the state chairman for nomination, since a party convention no longer chose the nominee.[2] The party conventions were often controlled by a unified party hierarchy headed by the state chairman.

As the newly elected chairman, Dickinson immediately began to assert his leadership. The majority of this committee consisted of young and ambitious men like Dickinson. Under his guidance the party leaders proposed to generate enthusiasm by organizing Democratic clubs in every town and ward in the state, no matter how few Democratic votes had been obtained in previous elections. "The young and vigorous men to the front" became the motto in the appointment of committees from the Congressional districts down to the smallest election precincts. The State Central Committee agreed that there should be no townships where the Republican candidate would run unopposed.

After the Democrats nominated Samuel J. Tilden as their presidential candidate in 1876, Dickinson, in personal consultation with him, mapped out the Michigan campaign. Dickinson found Tilden an able and intelligent political organizer: the latter knew what methods to employ to generate publicity and understood the psychology of advertising. That the young politician Donald Dickinson took some advice from this veteran campaigner seems obvious from a report in the *Detroit Free Press.* "No better indication could be had of the hopefulness with which the Democracy of Michigan has entered upon the work of regenerating the state than the zeal shown in circulating documents and literature."

In calling county conventions, Dickinson urged that the local leaders "invite all citizens irrespective of past party affiliations, who are opposed to continuing the corrupt rule of the past four years and to the control of bad men at the seat of government, to unite with us in the primaries held to elect delegates or nominate candidates." Dickinson reminded Republicans interested in reforming the party from within that Benjamin H. Bristow, "the candidate demanded of the late Republican convention by nine-tenths of the honest masses of the party," had received little support at the Republican convention. Dickinson challenged the Republican leaders to deny the as-

18

sertion that "the governing element of that Convention wanted no success for the party which would place at the head of government a positive, uncompromising and active foe of dishonest men and dishonest government."

Dickinson seemed to be a poised and polished politician when the state convention assembled in August in Detroit. At the opening session he informed the delegates that heretofore the caretaker had never allowed the Whitney Opera House to be used for a political gathering. Good-humoredly, Dickinson observed that he had assured the man that Democratic conventions behaved much better as a rule than church congregations. With introductions and formalities out of the way, the convention began the serious work of selecting a slate of nominees for the state ticket. William L. Webber, chairman of the Michigan delegation at the national convention in St. Louis, was chosen to head the ticket as the gubernatorial nominee. Hoping to send each delegate home in good spirits, Dickinson arranged an elaborate reception at his home the same evening. At this reception the delegates met those nominated for state offices during the day's proceedings. As the guests arrived, they passed through an entrance surrounded by huge flags. Within, the rooms were decorated with flags and flowers, and a large portrait of Tilden occupied a conspicuous place in the library. The exterior of Dickinson's home had been artistically trimmed with Chinese lanterns of red, white, and blue. Torch lights made the garden glow. To relax those with frayed nerves from the day's activities, the Twenty-second Infantry Band played well-chosen pieces of classical music.

The campaign gained momentum in September. The Democrats capitalized on the corruption surrounding the Grant administration and made reform the theme of their campaign. Specifically, the Democrats charged the Grant administration with whitewashing wrongdoers such as Secretary of War William W. Belknap, who had received bribes for the sale of trading posts in the Indian Territory, and Grant's private secretary, O. E. Babcock, who had been involved in the notorious Whiskey Ring. The Republicans had tried to usurp powers belonging to the state, said Alpheus S. Williams, Democratic congressman from Wayne County. "Federal bayonets are sent by the President into Sovereign states to overthrow legislatures and place partisan favorites in supreme authority, as was instanced in the state of Louisiana." In the same address Williams charged the federal government with squandering a great amount of money during the days of Grant.

In Detroit, Democrats gathered for the final political rally the evening before Election Day at the Detroit Opera House. Chairman Dickinson and other Democrats appeared confident. During the course of the evening Dickinson read messages from Abram S. Hewitt, chairman of the Democratic National Committee, and

19

Daniel Magone, chairman of the New York State Central Committee, assuring Michigan Democrats that New York would certainly place its electoral votes in the Tilden column. Magone confidently predicted: "I assure you that New York is as certain to cast her electoral vote for Tilden and Hendricks as the rising of tomorrow's sun."

Although Michigan gave her electoral votes to Republican presidential candidate Rutherford B. Hayes on Election Day, Dickinson could boast that Michigan achieved the distinction of making the largest Democratic gain in any one state in the Union. In 1872, Grant had polled 63.9 per cent of the popular vote in Michigan. In 1876, the electorate gave Hayes a little over 52 per cent of the popular vote. Tilden nearly doubled the total obtained by Greeley in 1872.

Dickinson contributed significantly to this impressive showing. Evidence of this came from the *Detroit Evening News*, which steered an independent course during the campaign. Although this newspaper was not particularly fond of Dickinson, it applauded Dickinson's campaign management. At the conclusion of the campaign the *Evening News* pointed out that, although Dickinson was being criticized by some in his own party because the Democrats had not won, this sniping was unjustified. "Never," said the *Evening News*, "was a political campaign in this state managed with more tact and energy than the recent one by Don M. Dickinson, esq., of this city, chairman of the Democratic State Central Committee. Had it resulted differently, and had the state been carried for Tilden, Mr. Dickinson's political fortune would have been made. As it is, the unfortunate chairman is only subjected to calumny and abuse. He was confident and sanguine, as every chairman should be, and now all lost bets are laid at his door."

Later the achievement of the Democratic organization in Michigan seemed even more astonishing when it became known that Dickinson had not asked for a dollar from the national committee. The national committee had requests for money from every state except Michigan. Dickinson explained that the money could better be spent in states which were more likely to vote Democratic than Michigan.

Dickinson remained chairman of the Democratic State Central Committee until July, 1878. Convinced that he had served long enough in this capacity, Dickinson resigned from the post after the Democratic state convention. At the convention Congressman Alpheus S. Williams complimented Dickinson, predicting that if the township organizations could be brought to the same relative degree of efficiency as the state organization, the Democratic party could carry Michigan by a five to ten thousand vote majority. Another

Democrat moved that the thanks of the convention be tendered to Dickinson for his services. The *Detroit Free Press* reported that "a unanimous rising vote showed the appreciation in which the retiring Chairman is held." Loud calls for a speech brought Dickinson to the platform to thank the convention for manifesting such good will toward him. Prolonged applause followed, prompting the *Free Press* to note that "the compliment paid to Mr. Dickinson is almost unprecedented."

Only two years later Dickinson no longer heard this kind of praise in his own Wayne County, although party stalwarts at the state level continued to draw on his talents. At the June state convention in 1880 they chose him to be a delegate-at-large to the national convention. When the time came for nominations, W. W. Duffield, a Dickinson supporter, seized the initiative. He recounted Dickinson's achievements and in conclusion boomed out, "For services well rendered, I present for your consideration the name of Don M. Dickinson." When Duffield had finished, two seconding speeches followed, and it appeared that the Dickinson bandwagon would roll to victory without difficulty. However, at this point Fred A. Baker from Wayne County gained the floor in an effort to stop Dickinson. Baker agreed that Dickinson had performed distinguished services, but that "it has been customary for Wayne County to have one of the four delegates-at-large, and I appeal to the justice of this convention and ask that you give us the man we want." The man that Wayne County wanted, said Baker, was not Donald M. Dickinson but Alexander W. Copland. After more oratory, the delegates voted. The state convention refused to endorse Wayne County's repudiation of Dickinson. Dickinson swamped his chief opponent by winning four hundred and forty votes to forty-eight for Copland.[3]

When the Democratic delegation from Michigan assembled at Cincinnati in late June, it chose Dickinson chairman of the Michigan delegation. In the pre-convention caucus to poll the delegates on their presidential preferences, the group split. Chairman Dickinson supported Supreme Court Justice Stephen J. Field, whereas most of the Michigan delegates leaned toward Henry B. Payne of Ohio. There still appeared to be some feeling of dissatisfaction with Dickinson within the Wayne County delegation, for a member from Dickinson's own district delivered a ringing endorsement of Samuel Tilden, the Democratic nominee in 1876, simultaneously blasting Field.

When Dickinson backed Field, some critics maintained that he was not sincerely interested in seeing the Justice nominated, but that he merely wished to forestall Tilden. This was not true, for Dickinson believed Justice Field to be a "great defender of constitutional liberty and the right of local and state government," even though Dickinson did not agree with all of Field's legal opinions. As for

Tilden, he did not believe that his health would permit him to wage another vigorous campaign. In his letter of withdrawal delivered to the national convention by his brother Henry, Tilden wrote: "Having now borne faithfully my full share of labor and care in the public service, and wearing the marks of its burdens, I desire nothing so much as an honorable discharge. I wish to lay down the honors and toils of even quasi party leadership, and to seek the repose of private life. . . ."

There were no strained feelings between Dickinson and the Tildens. In fact, Henry Tilden accompanied Dickinson to Detroit after the convention and was a guest in the Dickinson home for several days. Dickinson felt that the cordial relations established with Tilden during the 1876 campaign remained until the Governor's death in 1886.

The Democrats eventually nominated the old Civil War hero, Winfield S. Hancock. Hancock proved to be a better soldier than a political campaigner. He brought much criticism upon himself by calling the tariff a local question. The well-known cartoonist Thomas Nast depicted a bewildered Hancock asking a fellow Democrat, "Who is Tariff, and why is he for revenue only?" Although Hancock and his running mate, William H. English, an Indiana banker, were rather inept political leaders, the Democrats still came close to winning the presidency. Thus, in 1884, they looked with renewed hope to New York's governor, Grover Cleveland. Governor Cleveland achieved rising national prominence by giving his state honest leadership in the face of strong opposition from Tammany Hall. When Cleveland crossed swords with the machine by objecting to the renomination of their stalwart, Senator Thomas F. Grady, to the United States Senate, Democrats in several states began to see Cleveland as their strongest possibility for the presidency in 1884.[4] One of these Democrats was Donald Dickinson, now ready to take up the cudgel again.

Dickinson's star obviously was rising again when the state convention convened in June and named him chairman. At his best on occasions such as this, Dickinson launched an all-out attack on the Republican candidate, James Blaine. "A plumed knight! We remember when the feathers that he wore were plucked from a bird that was not white, a bird that is defined by the naturalists as one that feeds upon corruption and is called a vulture. We remember when his plumes were somewhat bedraggled. . . . We remember and have always remembered, that when this doughty champion of the nodding plumes has been weighed in the balance against hard cash, his manhood has always kicked the beam." Dickinson criticized the Republicans for picking a man like Blaine for their standard-bearer when that party had other men who "tower above James G. Blaine as Mount Washington rises above a wart. . . . Yet over the heads of these, ignoring all, this yelling concentration of small men at Chicago have raised up this strutting pigmy, a pigmy still."

Dickinson again had gained recognition as a prominent leader in Michigan politics. Although he did not seek the position, his name came to the fore as possible state chairman. The *Detroit Free Press* expressed the attitude of many Democrats. "The feeling on the whole is to confer the honor upon Mr. Dickinson in recognition of his splendid abilities and as a testimonial to the excellent work which he did for the Democracy when serving in that capacity in the Tilden campaign." In 1884, Dickinson desired the position of national committeeman from Michigan more than the chairmanship of the state Democratic organization. With Wayne County Democrats again solidly behind him, he had little difficulty becoming a national committeeman.

During the 1884 campaign Donald Dickinson exhibited none of the lackadaisical spirit displayed in the 1882 and even the 1880 campaigns. He organized meetings and used his oratorical talent to arouse enthusiasm among the rank and file. For example, late in October a political gathering described as the "greatest Democratic rally of the campaign" was held at White's Opera House in Detroit. Such prominent state Democrats as William P. Wells, Jerome Eddy, John G. Parkhurst and William Maybury were there. For the evening's festivities, the Democrats chose Dickinson to be chairman. Bubbling with enthusiasm, he pictured the Democratic party as an army fighting a crusade against a foe that stood for evil and corruption. Introducing Senator George H. Pendleton of Ohio, he remarked, "Three hundred and eighty thousand of the men of Ohio send you a greeting!" Dickinson realized that not the entire number were Democrats, but that they were all "friends and allies in the great contest we are waging against James G. Blaine and in aiding the election of Grover Cleveland." Continuing to portray the Democrats as a "grand army," Dickinson observed that the Republicans had been attacked and that Blaine, a false knight, had been driven "down the country roads and along the highways" and that he had been penned up "in the 'boodle' strongholds—the cities of Ohio." From reports that he had heard, Dickinson was very confident that Ohio would "assist in the triumphant election of Grover Cleveland and Thomas A. Hendricks. . . ." When the Senator had finished speaking, Dickinson continued to whip up the crowd to a greater degree of enthusiasm by calling for three cheers for Senator Pendleton that could be heard all the way to his home state of Ohio.

Also present at the rally was the father of General George Custer. The old man arose to receive a tremendous ovation from the crowd. When the aged father of General Custer had again found his seat,

Dickinson could not resist saying, "I have only to say that every drop of blood that flows from that heart and every beat of that heart is for Grover Cleveland."

Realizing the political worth of military heroes, Dickinson next turned to General W. S. Rosecrans. Reminding those present of Rosecrans' Civil War record, he introduced the old soldier in this manner. "Do you remember the first battle of the rebellion that we won—Rich Mountain—and who fought it? Do you remember the great means to that great end—the surrender of Lee? Do you remember the hero of the great Tennessee campaign? Do you remember Stone River?" By this time cries of "Rosy, Rosy" were heard from all sides, and Dickinson realized that he had performed his task of arousing the Democrats present to do battle eagerly during the last few days of the campaign.

On election eve Dickinson presided over the final Democratic rally in Detroit. Reports indicated that Democratic chances in 1884 were better than they had been for some time, and so Dickinson strode with eager anticipation onto a stage bedecked with flags and a huge Cleveland portrait. Before introducing the speakers for the evening, Dickinson himself made a few remarks. He told his audience that the *Detroit Post* had carried a story a few days before describing a reception which one thousand clergymen had accorded Blaine upon his return to New York. Actually, said Dickinson, only sixty-one of the thousand were genuine clergymen, for the servants had made a mistake and admitted all those who wore chokers and black coats. "As a result," said Dickinson, "we had there first and foremost the Reverend Jay Gould." Dickinson mentioned other Republican leaders that were present, facetiously prefacing each name with the title "Reverend." Finally, related Dickinson, Samuel D. Burchard, truly a clergyman, turned to Blaine and on behalf of the men of the cloth present, declared him "the representative of all virtues of this enlightened country, and that the other candidate represented the party of rum, Romanism and rebellion." Dickinson fully realized the Republican blunder, and, like a prize fighter striving to knock out a staggering opponent, he threw out this challenge to his Republican opponents: "Well, the party of rum, Romanism, and rebellion led by such men as Samuel J. Tilden, Winfield Scott Hancock, George William Curtis, John A. Andrew, and, coming nearer home, the Honorable George V. N. Lothrop and Ashley Pond will present its compliments tomorrow to the party of Boodle, Blasphemy and Blaine led by such leaders as Jay Gould ... and the rest of the Boodle gang. ..."

Attending this meeting was a former mayor of Detroit, William G. Thompson. Thompson had supported the Republican party most of his life, but he had switched his allegiance and vowed to vote for

24

Cleveland in 1884. When the throng shouted for Thompson, Dickinson replied, "You shall have him, you shall have him, but let me tell a story first." He then related a tale of a gentleman who, when crossing a bridge, fell into a morass. A servant ran for help shouting, "My master has fallen in." "How deep is he in?" came the reply. "Up to his ankles," reported the servant. "What are you yelling for, you fool?" questioned those who would help. "But he is in head first." Dickinson explained the parable: he recounted that William G. Thompson, knowing the dishonesty of James G. Blaine, could not vote for him, and "in coming over to us only meant to come to the depth of his ankles, but he has made a mistake and come over head first."

Election Day came, and on Thursday, November 6, the Detroit *Free Press* ran a picture with the caption, "We've Won." A strutting cock was pictured, and below the caption a smaller headline proclaimed, "The Tentacles of the Republican Octopus Loosened from the Ship of State." Actually on this Thursday those statements were premature, for the election hinged on returns being tabulated in the state of New York. No one was really certain which way New York would go.

Dickinson, determined to see that New York was not "stolen," hurriedly traveled to New York. In his pocket was a draft of fifty thousand dollars hastily collected in order to retain Roscoe Conkling, leader of the Stalwart faction in the Republican party.[5] Realizing that Roscoe Conkling was an implacable foe of Blaine, Dickinson immediately contacted him and gained his support. With Conkling alert and scrutinizing the election boards and ballot boxes of districts which would determine whether Blaine or Cleveland would win, there was little chance for dishonesty. Cleveland squeezed out a narrow victory in New York and with it won the presidency.

On Saturday night, November 8, the victorious Democrats in Michigan held what was termed "a big jollification meeting" at the Detroit Opera House. They were elated because only four of eleven Congressional districts were sending Republicans to Washington as a result of the Tuesday election. Although Michigan had not elected a Democratic governor, the Republicans were to be the minority party in the state legislature for the first time since the GOP's inception in 1854.

Dickinson had anticipated this moment for a long time. He had been only ten years old when the Democrats had last elected a President. Exuberantly he reminded his listeners that on election eve he had predicted that "the party of rum, Romanism, and rebellion would present its compliments next day to the party of Boodle, Blasphemy and Blaine." Said Dickinson tersely, "We have so paid our compliments." With sarcasm dripping from every word, he continued: "Jay Gould says he will concede Cleveland's election. Good, kind Jay Gould. He is like the ancient king who kindly granted his people the privilege of drawing their breath. We do not need Jay Gould's concession."

The year 1884 was a significant one for Grover Cleveland and the Democratic party. After many fruitless years, the Democrats had proved that they were still alive as a party and that they could still muster enough strength to elect a President. The two-party system which America had long cherished still existed and was given a formidable uplift through the election of Cleveland.

The year was no less significant in the life of Donald Dickinson. The election of Cleveland was to alter Dickinson's life considerably in the years ahead. By 1884, Dickinson had become a leading figure in Michigan politics, and with the election of Cleveland he became a leader in national politics. There is scant likelihood that he would have achieved such prominence had Cleveland lost in 1884.

Life was not all rosy for Dickinson during these years which saw this young lawyer "reaching the topmost round of the ladder" in politics as well as in his chosen profession. In 1878, sudden tragedy struck when the five Dickinson children died of spinal meningitis contracted during a summer vacation in Canada. Although the letters of Dickinson say little concerning these stunning blows, those who knew him and his wife reveal that it burdened the hearts of both for a long time. Excerpts from letters written by H. L. Holmes to Dickinson's mother after the deaths of these children reveal the anguish of the parents. "Had Don yet become reconciled? I trust that he feels by this time that his darlings are 'not lost'—only gone before." A few months later Holmes wrote concerning Mrs. Dickinson: "Fannie writes me she does not feel well these days and says it is hard work to compose her thoughts and write a letter."

Three years later this sorrow had not yet been erased, for a letter addressed to "Mother and dear ones at home" makes reference to this tragedy and indicates that the Dickinsons were still grieving. The writer promised to pray for Don and his wife and expressed the hope that they soon would find "sweet peace in resting on the strong arm of Jesus." The sympathizer was confident that "their darlings" were "safe in the arms" of Jesus and had "escaped the trials and temptations of the world." Of this the author was very confident, and he was certain also that it would be of comfort to "dear Don and Fannie if they would only believe."

What effect this tragedy had upon Dickinson and his career is difficult to judge. This crushing blow did not prevent him from pushing forward both as a politician and lawyer. It is evident from Dickinson's letters that he had a deep attachment for the two children, Frances and Donald, born after the early tragedy. He disliked being away from home for extended periods. This may explain to some degree his reluctance to accept a place in Cleveland's official family, for Dickinson now treasured those moments spent with the surviving members of his own family.

CHAPTER 3:

"I HAVE NOT LOST A PARTICLE OF MY CONFIDENCE IN YOU"

Grover Cleveland was the first Democratic President elected since James Buchanan. Long-suffering party faithful were elated by the victory and eager to share the spoils. Michigan politicians were no exception. Although unable to swing the Wolverine State into the Cleveland column, they, with the support of the Greenbackers, won seven of the eleven Congressional seats, leaving the Republicans with four members in the House and both Senate seats.

Traditionally, the President heeded the advice of the House members of his own party as far as postal appointments within the state were concerned, whereas senators had the primary influence in all other appointments. The new President, however, was to be his own man, as Professor Allan Nevins implied when he entitled his biography of Cleveland *A Study in Courage*. Cleveland was vitally interested in reform and refused to allow custom to constrain him. One prominent Democrat revealed that several Michigan congressmen expecting to share the spoils had formed a "machine for the purpose of squeezing various coveted offices out of the President." The Chief Executive quickly became aware of this and turned instead to Dickinson, "for the President and his friends in the Cabinet are intimately acquainted with his work and appreciate it as that of a man who holds the principles enunciated by the head of the government." Individuals suggested by Dickinson were named Ambassador to Russia, Governor of the Alaska Territory, Supreme Court justice in the Utah Territory, and Collector of Customs at Port Huron.[1] Because of Dickinson's increasing influence in matters of patronage, several members of the Michigan Democratic contingent in Washington resented him.

Shortly after the inauguration, Dickinson and William C. Maybury, leader of the Michigan Democrats in Congress, visited Cleve-

27

land in Washington. Maybury stated his request bluntly. He wished several federal appointments for people of his choice. Although Cleveland had just assumed office, the *Detroit Post* foresaw a rift developing between Maybury and Dickinson as it headlined the story of these Washington visits "Two Rivals." The concluding statement of this news story stated that, although Dickinson and Maybury had come to Washington together, they had kept "wide apart since they have been in the city."

Soon after the visits of Dickinson and Maybury, Cleveland made the first major federal appointment involving a Michigan man when he named Martin V. Montgomery of Lansing Commissioner of Patents. It was clearly a victory for Dickinson, who "had the honor to suggest the name of Mr. Montgomery." In an editorial entitled "Ave Caesar," the *Detroit Post* assessed this appointment: "The selection of Montgomery, if not Dickinson's work, is at least on Mr. Dickinson's side; and it looks very much as if Mr. Dickinson's new name was to be Boss."

Perhaps Dickinson's relationship with the President spurred Maybury into calling a meeting early in April of the eleven Democrats who had run for office in the state's Congressional districts the previous November. These eleven men met in Maybury's Washington office for the purpose of securing concerted action on various federal appointments. In order to exert as much pressure as possible, they agreed that any differences among them concerning appointments should be ironed out before approaching the President. Once a decision was reached, all would support it. Irked by Dickinson's influence, these Democrats intimated that they would not endure outside interference in the distribution of offices within their own particular districts. They made it clear to the President that they felt no one man in the state should be as influential as a senator in handing out federal appointments.

In May, 1885, the President surprised many citizens when he appointed George V. N. Lothrop of Detroit Ambassador to Russia. Michigan had been a Republican stronghold, and it was expected that such important posts would go to men from states that had been more faithful in supporting the Democratic party. In this nomination Dickinson's choice had again been favored. Later he wrote to Cleveland that the President's "own good judgment from your own impression of him made prompt use of the suggestion of the Lothrop name."

Although most important Michigan Democrats acclaimed the Lothrop appointment, the nomination of Orlando W. Powers of Kalamazoo to the Supreme Court of the Utah Territory evoked bitter opposition from the anti-Dickinson Congressional faction and actually ignited the simmering feud among Michigan Democrats. The Powers appointment came a month after Montgomery had been named Commissioner of Patents. Subsequent events and comments indicated that Powers had the full support of Dickinson, while Maybury and his followers were determined to frustrate Powers.

The *Detroit Post* reported that it had interviewed an unidentified Democrat who compared the Dickinson-Maybury relationship to that between Russia and England. These two nations, said this Democrat, were exchanging very courteous communications while at the same time preparing for war with each other. He termed any reports of political peace between Dickinson and Maybury as "absurd." Because the *Detroit Post* was not a pro-Dickinson organ, this newspaper's analysis of the Dickinson-Maybury feud is worth noting. The *Post* reported that certain prominent Democrats thought Dickinson had been presenting names of men who had been identified "with the Democratic party as workers rather than ... spoils seekers." Dickinson's nominees were competent, Democrats from principle, men "who have never trimmed or shifted with an eye to political preferment." They were the kind of men sought by Cleveland, and Dickinson, "in urging their claims, has an influence that the organizer and chief fugler in the ring can never acquire with the Administration."

Although Dickinson was gaining the upper hand in patronage decisions, he realized that his favored position was breeding jealousy and dividing the party. Therefore, in May, 1885, he wrote a letter to Cleveland hoping to rectify a situation that might do irreparable damage to the party in Michigan. Dickinson indicated to the President that "on precedent and authority," in the absence of a senator, a member of the National Committee and the chairman of the State Committee were considered as having the influence of senators in recommendations for all positions except the postmasterships. In spite of this, said Dickinson, "Mr. Eddy (the state chairman) and myself prefer that any and all precedents resting on machine methods be disregarded; and we are agreed that the competition for place should be open to all, and that, the question of fitness once settled, care should be taken to recommend those whose appointment would give satisfaction to the greater number of the locality to be affected."

Dickinson sought to smooth over differences. Although the traditional method of selection "was very objectionable" and had led to "much irritation among our people, yet the Congressional delegations have in the large majority of cases, presented candidates for petitions who are quite unobjectionable." Desiring to get the Michigan delegation behind the new administration, Dickinson urged that whenever the Congressional recommendations "would not work absolute demoralization at home, and injury and scandal to your administration, we prefer to concur with the delegation."

Efforts to heal the wounds failed. In June, the President appointed William L. Bancroft Collector of Customs at Port Huron over the protests of Ezra C. Carleton, representative from the district. The disgusted Carleton commented on Cleveland's action: "I endorsed the Michigan delegation's candidate and we were prepared to press our choice and oppose any other. . . . If he considers he is acting wisely in' rejecting the Congressmen and allowing himself to be governed by Mr. Dickinson, he must accept the results."

In October, the President favored Dickinson again by stating that "the time has now come to you when you are called upon to make a sacrifice for your country." Whereupon Cleveland offered Dickinson the post of Civil Service Commissioner. Cleveland explained that "this is the first offer I have made of the plan to any member of my party and I think it is the best position in the country to do good—to say nothing about gaining fame." Cleveland expected to reorganize the Civil Service Commission and place Dickinson at the head with "two first-rate assistants."

Dickinson was very pleased with Cleveland's note. Nevertheless, he sent a telegram to the President declining the position, since it might compromise the integrity of the administration. "In a vigorous and belligerent majority," Dickinson explained, "I have been to some extent a leader, not merely a strong and devoted Democrat, but a hard and a contentious partisan." Dickinson feared that his partisan record would hurt the cause of reform and discredit the President's program. "If through me," Dickinson wrote poignantly, "the slightest reflection should be cast upon this administration, I shall want to die."

As 1885 wore on, the lines hardened between Dickinson and the Congressional delegation. Congressmen most strongly opposed to Dickinson included Congressmen Maybury, Carleton, and Charles Comstock of Grand Rapids. Comstock fretted, "My advice has sometimes been asked for and at all times been ignored except when not opposed by Dickinson." This congressman accused Cleveland of ignoring "the chosen Representatives of the people" and considered it "as great an insult to the constituency as to the members of Congress." A missive from Dickinson to Cleveland in December, 1885, indicates that relations between Dickinson and his opponents had become more embittered. Opposition centered around the Powers and Bancroft appointments. Earlier in the year Dickinson had sought to minimize his differences with the congressmen, but the spirit of conciliation now seemed to evaporate as Dickinson came to the defense of Bancroft. To evaluate Bancroft's standing in Michigan, Dickinson suggested "the most unfavorable test for him." He explained to Cleveland that Bancroft "has been a strong partisan and is politically hated by leaders of the Republican party." Nonetheless, Dickinson predicted that if Cleveland were to call in either or both Republican senators from Michigan, "you will, I am sure, find that nothing unfavorable can be said." The party could afford to have a Republican Senate reject Bancroft, but "it cannot afford to have the Representatives of our first success discredit him within the party. This would create a want of confidence in the stability of things, in the steadiness of decision which would be disastrous."

Midterm elections were to be held in 1886. The Democrats realized that this election would be significant in indicating the reaction of citizens to the first Democratic administration in many years. With this in mind, one might have expected a closing of the ranks so that the Democrats would have every chance of making a good showing in November.

This was not the case. The year opened with the split in Democratic ranks as wide as ever. In January, Edwin F. Conely, the Democrat who had strongly opposed Dickinson's original choice for the presidential nomination in 1880, testified before the Senate Judiciary Committee against the confirmation of Orlando Powers as a judge of the Supreme Court of Utah. There was a general feeling that he had gone as "the representative of the Michigan Congressmen who did not fancy the way Don M. Dickinson was manipulating appointments." The friction increased so that many appointments not only by the federal government but also within the state Democratic party were considered victories or defeats by one side or the other. For instance, when Jerome Eddy resigned as chairman of the State Central Committee in March, 1886, the party chose John J. Enright to fill his spot. This was a triumph for Dickinson, as he and Enright were close associates.

During the first year of the Cleveland administration, it seemed that Donald M. Dickinson could not lose. However, in April, nearly a year after Orlando Powers' nomination to Utah's Supreme Court, the President withdrew his name. This was a major setback for Dickinson, since he not only had recommended Powers but had continued to back him in the face of considerable opposition. Most interesting is the newspaper comment concerning the withdrawal of Powers' name. Powers was the principal in this affair, but the editors attached greater significance to the effect the withdrawal would have upon Dickinson's position as a presidential confidant.

There can be little doubt that Dickinson was disheartened by this turn of events. Nonetheless, if the newspapers had had access to a letter sent by Cleveland to Dickinson in February, there would have been less speculation regarding the Cleveland-Dickinson relationship. When the President began to realize that Powers would probably not be confirmed, he intimated that he was prepared to withdraw the name of Powers and "appoint another good Michigan name, if you approve." The President concluded this message with a statement that must have been some consolation to Dickinson: "Whatever happens I beg you to believe that I have not lost a particle of my confidence in you."

After Dickinson refused the chairmanship of the Civil Service Commission, Cleveland realized that the Michigan Democrat was not seeking any government post for himself. However, the President desired to show concretely that his relations with Dickinson had not been strained by the Powers affair. In May, he appointed him to the coveted honorary position as visitor to the Naval Academy. As a member of the Board of Visitors, Dickinson made occasional visits to Annapolis in order to inspect the Naval Academy. This appointment, said the *Free Press*, "is an exceedingly graceful recognition of the esteem in which he is held by the President."

Though Cleveland may have held Dickinson in high regard, many Michigan Democrats did not share this sentiment, and the intramural fight continued throughout the summer. In early August, Congressman Carleton, who had opposed the nomination and confirmation of William L. Bancroft, met defeat in his bid for renomination at the hands of a Dickinson stalwart, Elliot Stevenson. As the *Evening News* phrased it, "Congressman Carleton's scalp has been taken by Don M. Dickinson's local brave, Elliot G. Stevenson." This embittered Lewis F. Atkin, who had directed and organized Carleton's campaign for re-election. Atkin predicted that a split in the ranks for the Carleton supporters "will not support Mr. Stevenson or any other figurehead for Mr. Dickinson."

The anti-Dickinson Democrats railed at their erstwhile leader. A former Democratic senator from Michigan charged that "Dickinson has neither official position, statesmanship, political influence nor experience that entitles him to such overmastering influence with the appointing power, especially in opposition to the wishes of those chosen by the people to represent them." Nathaniel E. Stewart, a Democratic politician from Kalamazoo who had hoped to share in the spoils after Cleveland's 1884 victory, was another outspoken critic of Dickinson. He believed that Dickinson had caused the congressmen to be made "laughing stock." "He has belittled them in every way possible. He has built up a Dickinson dynasty—a Dickinson hierarchy—and has sought to make himself dictator." Foster Pratt, Democratic State Chairman during the 1872 Greeley campaign, also aligned himself against Dickinson. To embarrass Dickinson he published the letter Dickinson had written after the 1872 campaign vowing never to support the party again.

Although Dickinson did lose a battle when the Senate rejected the nomination of W. L. Bancroft as Collector of Customs at Port Huron, his forces were regaining control of the Democratic state organization. In August, the Wayne County convention met for the purpose of selecting delegates to the state Democratic convention. The *Detroit Evening News*, more sympathetic with Maybury than Dickinson, admitted that "the county convention was as thoroughly controlled by Mr. Dickinson's friends as if that gentleman had appointed every man who sat in it." The convention proceedings prove the point, since a Dickinson man won the chairmanship, and Dickinson himself gained the coveted portfolio of leader of the county delegation to the state convention.

One week later the state Democratic convention convened in Grand Rapids, and the test of strength resumed between the two factions. On the basis of a news leak from the State Central Committee, the independent *Evening News* predicted that the convention would not fully endorse the Cleveland administration. Another news source carried the same rumor and added that "Cleveland's amazement at news of this sort from the home of Mr. Don M. Dickinson will simply be overwhelming and he cannot fail to construe it as significant of the action of the state in the national Democratic convention in 1888."

Dickinson worked hard to avert this disaster. The evening before the convention he was the "central figure of the Democratic hosts." Drawing on all of his political cunning, he greeted rural delegates with a handshake and a "hello, there." The gesture was cordial, but at the same time not "slopping over," and created good will among those who would be transacting business the next day.

Dickinson's preparations paid off as his peers elected him permanent chairman. With the prerogatives of this powerful post, Dickinson could undermine the incipient revolt against the administration and gain an outright Cleveland endorsement. Thus, in his opening remarks as chairman, he mentioned that he had listened to the invocation with "bowed head and responsive heart," but there was one sentiment the "revered gentleman" had failed to utter—"one sentiment upon a subject about which I shall have nothing more to say, and that was, I say to this convention of Democrats, God bless, save, and keep that Democrat of Democrats, the noblest one of them all, Grover Cleveland, President of the United States." The convention delegates got the message and endorsed the Cleveland administration without reservation.

Friends and opponents realized that Dickinson had won the day. The *Evening News*, which earlier in the week hinted that the convention might not endorse Cleveland and thus rebuke Dickinson as well, was forced to admit that Dickinson was a "bigger man" than Zachariah Chandler, the man who had controlled the Republican organization in Michigan for many years. That Dickinson was entirely satisfied with the actions of the convention was quite apparent when it was announced the next day that the 1886 campaign fund had been started by a five-thousand-dollar contribution from none other than Donald M. Dickinson.

Although Election Day was less than three months away, intra-party strife continued. About a week after the state convention a news story, headlined "Don Is Boss," announced the withdrawal of William Maybury from the race for renomination to Congress. Maybury had expected a third term but realized that the Dickinson forces had carried the day. "The situation in this district, if I may judge from what I hear," Maybury declared, "precludes the possibility of the honor of a third candidacy devolving on me without an unseemly contest, awakening bitter animosities and jealousies."

In September, the Wayne County Democrats chose Judge John Logan Chipman to be the candidate for the House in Maybury's place. Dickinson was instrumental in effecting a compromise between those who had supported Maybury and those, like himself, who wanted John Enright. Though independent, Chipman thought like Dickinson on many issues. Thus, Dickinson was quite willing to stand beside Edwin Conely, one of Maybury's staunchest supporters, and address the convention in the way of an old Roman orator: "Friends of the brotherhood of Democrats: If any loose hatchets remain unburied, here, let them be buried. All honor to Maybury and Enright for burying their differences. It is a noble act. It will give us the state ticket. I am authorized to state in behalf of Enright that if there is a Democrat here who has been his enemy, up to this time, being a Democrat he is his friend. I can say for myself that if there is any man here who up to this time has been my enemy, if he is a Democrat, he is my friend." With this he shook hands with Conely and continued, "It was a noble concession on the part of both the young men. Any position or honor that may be given to either William C. Maybury or John J. Enright will be an honor to the Democratic party. To your tents, gentlemen and Democrats; let us carry the district, let us carry the legislature, and let us carry the state."

On the eve of Election Day the Democrats held a large rally which Dickinson chaired. During the course of the evening a letter addressed to Dickinson was read expressing the hope that the Democrats on the morning of November 2 could "point with pride to the leaders of the Republican party and say to them, 'Behold the sun of Austerlitz.' "

On Election Day, however, Dickinson could not play the role of a victorious Napoleon. Republicans nearly swept the state, winning the gubernatorial race, both state houses, and a majority of the Congressional seats. Democrats sought to minimize the defeat. Dickinson observed that the margin of victory—7,000 votes—was small "when in old time the State gave from 25,000 to 60,000 majority" to the Republicans. He pointed out that the Republicans had brought in their big guns—Senators John Sherman and Henry Blair in addition to James G. Blaine himself. The Democrats, on the other hand, had "made a purely domestic fight without a man or a cent from outside." Moreover, the Republican "desperation and demoralization" was shown by "their fusion with Knights of Labor, Greenbackers and free traders in my district and elsewhere."

State Democratic Chairman I. M. Weston pointed out that 1886 is the "off year in politics. As a rule, elections go against every administration two years after it is put into power." Disharmony in Democratic ranks also took its toll, said Weston. While Dickinson minimized this—"there was some inevitable straining of relations in the changes about offices, but this always occurs"—Weston attributed more importance to these intraparty squabbles. "Unfortunate differences and jealousies over the nominations in two or three of our Congressional districts contributed largely to reduce our vote." He specifically mentioned the Sixth District where Congressman Carleton's unsuccessful bid for renomination had occasioned recriminations.

Weston's view that disharmony did cost votes seems to be a more accurate appraisal than Dickinson's. The least partial of the Detroit papers, the *Evening News*, substantiated Weston's analysis. In a lengthy editorial entitled "It Might Have Been," the *Evening News* reminded its readers of an open letter that it had addressed to Maybury and Dickinson. In this letter the Detroit newspaper expressed the belief that the Dickinson-Maybury quarrel threatened to divide the party and called for peace between the two factions, for "neither side can 'down' the other except by 'downing' the party at the same time. Each has plenty of faithful friends who will stick to the bitter end, and lower their flag, if the fight continues, only in mutual destruction."

There was some speculation that the Democratic setback would end the political influence of Don Dickinson. Weston was queried regarding this and replied that he had "a large scrap book at home nearly filled with regular political obituaries of Dickinson." He was confident that, just as these dire pronouncements had been incorrect before, they would be at this time.

It soon became apparent that Weston's observation was correct. When the 1887 legislative session opened in January, many Democrats wished to reveal that they still regarded Dickinson highly by making him their nominee for United States senator. Dickinson, however, strongly requested that this not be done. In February, he gained the honor of escorting a number of prominent Democrats to Washington in order to introduce them to President Cleveland.

As far as Cleveland was concerned, Dickinson remained a trusted advisor and an able lieutenant. Early in 1887, Congress passed the Interstate Commerce Act. Cleveland wanted Michigan's Thomas M.

Cooley to become the first chairman of the Interstate Commerce Commission. Cooley had acquired a national reputation as a distinguished jurist: he possessed the kind of character that would be necessary in a position where he would face much opposition. Cleveland was confident that the people would have much trust in the administration of the law if Cooley accepted the position.

When Cleveland decided that Cooley was the man he wanted, he still had to persuade Cooley to accept. For this task he selected Don Dickinson. In February, Dickinson visited Cooley at his home. After the visit Dickinson immediately wrote a letter to the President expressing Cooley's reluctance, but he concluded that Cooley would accept if Cleveland appointed him. With this assurance, Cleveland tendered the position to Cooley, sincerely entreating, ". . . I earnestly ask you to consent to serve us all in the capacity mentioned." Cooley could not refuse the President's call.

* * * * * *

The election of Cleveland in 1884 marked the beginning of a long association between Dickinson and Cleveland. As time went on, an acquaintance based on mutual interest gradually ripened into a friendship that continued until Cleveland's death in 1908.

Several factors cemented the bond between these two men. Both, of course, were vitally interested in politics and the Democratic party. Cleveland recognized Dickinson's abilities as a politician and appreciated his efforts in recreating a vigorous Democratic party in Michigan.

Allan Nevins points out that "men expected Cleveland to display not an excursive boldness, but simply a greater honesty and earnestness than his predecessors, and he understood this perfectly." Cleveland himself summed up his philosophy on this subject when he said, "Let us be steadfast in our beliefs, unmoved by clamor; and untempted by an inordinate desire for success at any cost of principle and consistency. Thus will we serve our country best; thus shall we know the joy that mere success can never know."

Cleveland possessed an unreserved courage, and he saw in Dickinson the same courage and conviction. Thus, in seeking men who would symbolize reform in his administration, Cleveland turned to persons like Dickinson, William F. Vilas of Wisconsin, William C. Endicott of Massachusetts, and Allen G. Thurman of Ohio.

There were other traits that Cleveland found in Dickinson which helped to mold bonds that would last a lifetime. Both were energetic, untiring workers driven on to accomplish successfully their desired goals. Their careers ran parallel in many ways: both had chosen the legal profession as their vocation; both enjoyed the challenges that this work presented and strove to meet these challenges boldly. At the same time, neither could resist the lure of the world of politics. Both enlisted at an early age under the banner of the Democratic party and both were successful in climbing to positions of prominence. While Cleveland had risen from ward supervisor in Buffalo, New York to President of the United States, Dickinson had moved from substitute on the Michigan State Central Committee in 1872 to a nationally recognized Democratic leader at the time of Cleveland's election.

Both Dickinson and Cleveland also adhered to a rather strict Jeffersonian view of limited government. Dickinson as an attorney argued against federal court encroachment upon state courts. He feared that too much government would injure the common citizen in America. Dickinson sounded much like Jefferson when he said: "Democratic principles are the principles which must govern this land; the greatest good to the greatest number; domestic self-government and the striking down of John Adams' theory that men are divided into two classes, gentlemen and simple men. . . ." He believed that the Democratic party had always been "the protector and safeguard of the American system of government, of personal liberty and of private rights guaranteed by the Constitution and of local self-government," which Dickinson considered "the safety of our system."

Cleveland, too, was a Jeffersonian Democrat in that he feared government that became too centralized. He said in one message to Congress: "Our mission among the nations of the earth, and our success in accomplishing the work God has given the American people to do, require of those intrusted with the making and execution of our laws perfect devotion, above all other things, to the public good. This devotion will lead us to resist strongly all impatience of constitutional limitations of Federal power, and to check persistently the increasing tendency to extend the scope of Federal legislation into the domain of State and local jurisdiction, upon the plea of subserving the public welfare. The preservation of the partitions between proper subjects of Federal and local care and regulation is of such importance under the Constitution, which is the law of our very existence, that no consideration of expediency or sentiment should tempt us to enter upon doubtful ground."

Common interests and sympathetic ideas regarding the philosophy and nature of government were instrumental in drawing these two men together. However, all of this might not have created a lasting friendship had either man possessed traits repulsive to the other. Quite the opposite was true: Cleveland respected the judgment and good sense of Dickinson, and he consulted him increasingly over the years. Although Cleveland was President, he treated Dickinson as an equal. As has been seen, Dickinson had a great deal of influence on federal patronage in Michigan. In such matters Cleveland appears to have had implicit faith in Dickinson even after some of the appointments had been vigorously assailed. Cleveland appreciated the manner in which Dickinson rendered advice. The President never felt harried by Dickinson; the President usually sought out Dickinson when he wished his counsel.

In turn, Dickinson never forgot that Cleveland was the "Great Chief." However, he did not become a mere puppet—something Cleveland would have despised. When Dickinson became convinced that his own position was right, he vigorously defended it. At the same time, Dickinson labored to prevent friction within his party when a just compromise could be effected. These characteristics and traits were revealed early in the Cleveland-Dickinson relationship and help to explain this enduring friendship.

CHAPTER 4:

"COMING DOWN THERE"

During the early months of the Cleveland administration, Donald Dickinson resisted the President's attempts to entice him into a government position. He once mentioned that he was "going out of politics." Nonetheless, he explained to Cleveland that "by 'going out of politics' I do not mean that I would not at any time, under any circumstances of personal sacrifice, by night as well as by day, serve the President." He simply believed he could better aid Cleveland out of office rather than by "coming down there," as the President phrased it. Cleveland, however, refused to accept this as Dickinson's final word, and in 1887 persuaded him to take the position of postmaster general after William F. Vilas, the former postmaster, moved to the Interior Department.

Dickinson's fierce loyalty and devotion to Cleveland compelled him to accept the cabinet portfolio, although he had sufficient reason to decline. As one of the nation's foremost lawyers, his salary was several times the eight thousand dollars he would earn as postmaster general; Dickinson refused to supplement his salary by practicing law while in the cabinet, since he wished to devote all his time to his new position. "All my private matters have been sacrificed," he wrote to a client some months later, "and I have been unable to give the slightest attention to private business since I have been here." Dickinson was also reluctant to leave Michigan for an extended period at a time when he could do much to reinvigorate the party in Michigan. "Since I have been here, I have had many requests, including a large number from gentlemen in whom I took no special interest, and some from those to whom I was very warmly attached. To all those I have invariably replied that, at my distance, I could not form a judgment as to what was best; that it would be in the highest degree improper for me, occupying the position I do under the Federal administration, to attempt to influence local action."

Perhaps the feelings of both Cleveland and Dickinson concerning this appointment are best summed up in one of Dickinson's letters. In it he told the President that if the decision to appoint him to "this high place" had been motivated by a desire to honor him, he "would positively decline. At this time," said Dickinson, "I need hardly deliberate when you already so well understand that the confidence alone which you have in me fills the highest measure of my desires and ambitions." He felt that he owed "no higher duty than that I owe you and all you represent" and that if the President still thought it advisable that he accept the position in spite of what had been said, "I must then consider your judgment conclusive of what is best." To this Cleveland replied with no hesitation, "I have settled the matter in my favor and in favor of the country and shall look for you at the time already indicated." Thus, Cleveland nominated Dickinson in December, 1887, and the Senate confirmed the nomination on January 16, 1888.

Cleveland's conviction that Dickinson would place the interests of the public first explains the President's persistence. An occurrence shortly before the confirmation illustrated Dickinson's concern. The new postmaster general was quite upset by the behavior of a day watchman in the Post Office Department. Failing to recognize Dickinson, the watchman was very curt when Dickinson sought entrance to the department after two o'clock, the time the department was closed to the public. When Dickinson said that he had business, the watchman replied, "I said it was closed." "Don't know," was the answer to a question concerning how admission might be obtained. When asked regarding the time that one could enter the next day, the watchman retorted, "You will have to find out for yourself, sir." A short time later Dickinson called the watchman into his office. Recognizing his *faux pas*, the stunned public servant nevertheless mustered his courage and defended his actions by saying that ". . .so many men come that we are greatly annoyed and become very tired." But Dickinson brushed the excuse aside. "That is undoubtedly true, but you should remember that the government pays you for being annoyed. . . . I would have very much preferred that you had offended a Senator than to have failed to be courteous to the veriest stranger that ever asked admission to the department."

Dickinson faced his biggest challenge as postmaster general less than two months after taking office. This crisis began on February 27, 1888, when locomotive engineers and firemen on the Chicago, Burlington, and Quincy Railroad went on strike. Dickinson and the

Post Office Department became involved when it seemed that the transportation of mail would be seriously hampered by this strike. The situation threatened to become more serious when the possibility arose that engineers and firemen from other railway companies would refuse to handle cars belonging to the Chicago, Burlington, and Quincy system.

The railroad owners hoped that the United States government would break the strike by insisting upon the transportation of mail. Dickinson, however, gave no indication that such action was contemplated; so the railroads appealed to him for action: "We come before the Post Office Department in order that we may have a fair understanding as to what we may expect in the future." In his reply Dickinson made clear exactly where he stood on this matter. He began in a friendly but firm tone indicating that an efficient mail service rested primarily on cordial cooperation between the Post Office and the owners and operators of the railroad companies. At the same time he thought it "a grave defect in our system" that the railroad companies were not compelled to carry the mail by law.

The one lever the Post Office Department had was the right of the postmaster general to levy fines and deductions "for every failure to perform service whether from fault or from unavoidable accident." Dickinson believed the intent of this legal remedy was to cajole, not to punish. He would not exercise these powers "to their utmost limits." At the same time he hoped this force would be "wholesomely respected."

When Dickinson spoke of failing to press the power to impose fines and deductions to the limit, he cited examples of this. He did not believe that railroads should be fined if mails were delayed by reason of an act of God, such as a heavy blizzard. Besides this, Dickinson said, "I am of the opinion that no fine or deduction should be imposed for delay caused by a broken axle, hot box, or any similar accident against which, in the common knowledge of railroading, the highest degree of diligence and care have not been able to guard against." On the other hand, Dickinson reminded the railway companies of their duties, asserting that "thousands of people and thousands of interests depend or are involved in the delivery of the mails. The passenger traffic or freight of a single train involve infinitesimal interests in comparison with a heavy mail and must in no case be given precedence. . . . " Dickinson firmly asserted that if railway companies disregarded this philosophy, "the penalty in such cases should be heavy enough to make it thoroughly understood and remembered."

The chief matter that interested the company was the government's attitude toward a strike against a railway company. Dickinson answered this bluntly, stating, "I do not conceive that a strike of railroad employees can afford any excuse for failure to carry the

40

mails. There has been no case where men and facilities could not be found sufficient to carry the mails; and if cases occur where the contractors either will not or cannot take other business in addition, it can be no ground for refusal or failure to proceed with the Government business alone."

Thus, under Dickinson, the Post Office Department refused to get involved in any strike other than to insist that there should be no interference with the mail and the transportation of it. It was the responsibility of the employer and the employee to work out a mutually acceptable agreement. The government had no obligation to pay special compensations to the railroad companies because of inconveniences created by the strike.

During this period Dickinson's words and actions had been carefully observed by citizens throughout the United States. If one can judge policy by results, Dickinson acted properly, for the mail got through without resort to force or court injunctions even though the Burlington strike continued until January, 1889. Congressman William L. Scott complimented him by saying that Dickinson had handled the matter "very ably." He elaborated, "It was an extremely delicate matter to handle and it required great tact on his part to accomplish what he has done in establishing the precedent that any railroad having a contract with the Government for the transportation of the mails is bound to transport them and to afford the public proper mail facilities on its line."

Dickinson contested the big corporations again on the matter of subsidies. The Senate amended the Postal Appropriations Bill, providing an $800,000 subsidy to steamship companies carrying the mail to South and Central American ports and those in the West Indies. Dickinson vigorously opposed such a subsidy, for he believed that it would benefit only a few large corporations while harming the interests of all others using the mails. Therefore, he hoped to persuade the House to reject the amendment. In a lengthy letter to Chairman James H. Blount of the House Committee on Post Offices and Postroads, he indicated why this amendment should not be passed. He explained that even without the subsidy mail steamers had numerous benefits, such as the right to discharge their cargoes immediately, to sail at any hour of the day or night, and never to be detained on any pretext. The postmaster general declared that preference had been given to American ships. However, there were times when foreign ships had to be employed on the principle that "the first duty of the department to our citizens under the law was to give them the best, most expeditious and certain mail facilities within its resources." The legislation proposed would limit the postmaster general "to contract with American built or American registered steamships for the transportation of mails to the parts of Central and South America and the West Indies for a period of not

41

less than five years, and with a compensation for each outward trip of one dollar per mile." This would stifle any competition. "In the present conditions," said Dickinson, "the proposed law might as well name the few persons to whom this money is paid." He stated that the proposed legislation "would seem to exclude the exercise of any power of any representative of this government to provide for this mail service in the interest of the people. . . ." This was contrary to Dickinson's sense of justice, for he believed that the Post Office Department "should be independent and should at all times be enabled to send the mails by the most expeditious routes, and make use of the best facilities afforded for that purpose from among all carriers offering."

Bearing in mind that the Post Office Department belonged to all the people, Dickinson presented statistics revealing the cost of the subsidy. Poorer service would result if foreign ships could not be employed. Concluded Dickinson, ". . . I feel confident that such administration will result only in a very great pecuniary benefit to a dozen individuals at the expense and embarrassment of good service, and of inconvenience, injustice and material injury to the great body of the people whose money will be used in the purchase of those results."

After carefully following debate on this bill, Dickinson wrote another more personal message to Chairman Blount. He noted that Senator Preston B. Plumb had made the statement that the subsidy amendment "left it discretionary with me to contract for less than the amount of one dollar per nautical mile." Dickinson, however, found that he would have no power to negotiate for less because of the mandatory provision to contract "with the men that will see that I am compelled to pay them the maximum." Previously, foreign ships could be contracted, but the proposed legislation would prohibit such contracts. Dickinson compared this situation to that of a farmer who proposed to test his son, a college graduate, concerning his knowledge of business. This farmer sent his son to town to buy a cow, instructing him to pay no more than twenty-five dollars if possible, but to go as high as fifty if necessary. The son went to the owner of the cow, who immediately asked how much the boy would give for the animal. He told the owner that he would like to pay twenty-five dollars, but if he could not get it for that sum, he would go as high as fifty dollars. "It is needless to say," concluded Dickinson, "that the bargain was struck at the maximum figure."

The senators finally buckled under Dickinson's withering attack and dropped the rider. "Senators Surrender" trumpeted the *Detroit Free Press* in its leading news story. "Postmaster General Dickinson is the David that slew the subsidy Goliath."

Reform received another boost when Dickinson issued an order placing employees of the Railway Mail Service under civil service.

42

This order, dispatched on the last day of December, 1888, went into effect in May, 1889. The Civil Service Commission believed this amendment to be one of "the most important made in the rules during the year."[1]

Steps that the Post Office Department took under Dickinson to improve service included the signing of parcel post conventions with British Honduras and Mexico. The first parcel post convention concluded by the United States with any foreign country had gone into operation shortly before Dickinson took office. Under Dickinson these agreements were expanded to the countries mentioned, while plans were made to conclude conventions with more South and Central American neighbors, so that the time would soon come "when the 'Three Americas' will be embraced in one grand parcel post union." The convention with Mexico was especially important. Prior to the parcel post convention no one could send through the mails any article of merchantable value between the United States and her southern neighbor. It was believed that the parcel post convention would do much to strengthen trade relations between the United States and Mexico.

In his efforts to correct abuses arising from the franking privilege, Dickinson was not successful. He soon discovered that unauthorized persons were using the franking privilege. In some instances congressmen seemed to allow the unauthorized use of their franking privileges, while in other cases certain individuals were forging the names of those authorized to use it.

In February, 1888, Dickinson came to grips with this delicate problem and sent a message to the president of the Senate, saying, "The right to send matter in the mails under unofficial frank has by recent legislation been considerably extended, and opportunity largely increased for the abuse of this privilege." Dickinson explained that "the placing of official names upon public or private matter by others than the officers on whom the right is conferred is easy, difficult of detection by postal officials, and under present statutes not explicitly declared punishable." To eliminate the abuse he suggested that the franking privilege be abolished. In its place Dickinson proposed that a yearly allowance be given to each senator and representative for the purchase of postage stamps, which would place each one "upon an exact equality." No one would be allowed to use services without charge beyond his allowance.

Dickinson's proposal on this touchy subject made no headway. Apparently, the members of Congress wanted no intrusion, for no attempts were made to introduce legislation along the lines that Dickinson suggested

Although Dickinson was postmaster general for a period of less than fourteen months, he was able to forge a much closer personal bond with Cleveland. Prior to this time Dickinson had met Cleveland several times, but it usually had been in order to discuss business. When Dickinson became postmaster general, there was opportunity for informal visits or outings in addition. For instance, the two men frequently went fishing together. This constant association, both officially and unofficially, turned what formerly had been chiefly a business relationship into one that was warmer and more intimate.

Dickinson thought his experience as postmaster general allowed him to make two suggestions which he termed "radical reforms in postal administration." Shortly after his retirement from the office he published an article in the *North American Review* entitled "Progress and the Post," outlining these suggestions.[2] The first reform proposed provided for a "distribution of the powers and responsibilities of the post-office establishment." He explained that "no agency of government, state, national, or municipal, so touches the individual citizen in domestic affairs and in his going and in his coming" as the Post Office Department. Yet this agency had no officials near the people who had enough authority and responsibility to effect better service when it was necessary. All complaints of service had to go to Washington to be remedied. Dickinson proposed to correct this situation with a reorganized system of territorial divisions whose heads would be clothed with the power and responsibilities which at the time only the postmaster general possessed. In policy matters relating to the more universal interests of the country the postmaster general would remain the superior.

Dickinson's second suggestion stemmed from his experience in dealing with strike-threatened railway companies which were under contract to carry the mail. During his tenure there had been no serious interruptions of mail service, but Dickinson could foresee dangerous possibilities unless the laws were altered. "It is a startling proposition," he wrote, "that the only alternative, in case any great trunk line should refuse to renew its contract for carriage, is that set out in the act of Congress, hereafter quoted, which authorizes the Postmaster General in such case to send forward the mails by 'horse-express, or otherwise'!" He believed that Congress had the constitutional authority to compel a railroad company to keep a contract. Failure to transport the mail was contrary to public interests, and "when one devotes his property to a use in which the public has an interest, he, in effect, grants to the public an interest in that use and must submit to be controlled by the public for the common good to the extent of the interest he has thus created."

In spite of what had occurred, Dickinson concluded that "it may still require a few more striking illustrations of the fact that the railroad carrier, and not the Government, is master of the situation, to transform the suggestion for revision, frequently presented to Congress, into an imperative demand from the source of power." Had Dickinson's last suggestion been heeded, many of the difficulties incurred during the 1894 Pullman strike might have been averted.

As postmaster general, Dickinson played a less conspicuous role in the 1888 political campaign even though he desired to become more involved. Soon after the Senate had approved his nomination, he wrote, "You cannot conceive of how anxious I am about the Senate. . . . I do not think we at home have appreciated the space which Michigan occupies in the mind of the Great Chief, or comprehended the hope for support from her which is grounded upon the intelligence and honesty of our people." In the same letter he complained of "this harness on my back," which he felt would hamper him in the 1888 campaign.

Because of his position as postmaster general and because he wished to give the Republicans no opportunity to reproach the Cleveland administration in the matter of reform, Dickinson did not attend the Democratic convention. He explained that, although there was actually nothing to forbid a federal official from "the exercise of his individual influence as a citizen in favor of the views which he holds in the same manner as if he were not in office, yet, in view of the disgraceful abuses heretofore adverted to, it is a matter which suggests itself to the good taste and judgment of sensible men, whether the indecencies heretofore practiced should even seem to be imitated by the appearance of Federal officials of this Administration at conventions."

At the same time Dickinson did what he could to quash efforts to place his name before the national convention as a candidate for Vice President. There was some speculation that he would be nominated for the position. One New York journal came out strongly for him. Michigan Democrats wished to endorse him for the vice presidency, but he insisted that the Michigan delegation go uninstructed on this matter to the national convention. He wrote a letter to one supporter saying, "I am sorry it would give you pleasure to see me commit such a folly as to be a candidate for that place. . . ." He continued by avowing that no higher honor could be conferred upon him than that of being an individual in whom the President had confidence. He already had been given this honor from a man whom he called "the foremost figure of the time."

The fact that Dickinson had been named to Cleveland's cabinet enhanced his stature among Michigan Democrats. Even though he believed that he could not be as active as he might have were he not postmaster general, he remained the state's leading Democrat. On May 3, the Wayne County Democratic convention resolved "that the President did credit to himself and honor to the state of Michigan and especially Wayne County when he appointed as Postmaster General Don M. Dickinson." One week later the Democratic state convention meeting in Grand Rapids passed a similar resolution.

Dickinson did make a limited number of campaign appearances prior to the election. In late September, he made his first official excursion to Michigan since moving to Washington. The occasion was a huge political rally held in Detroit where he was scheduled as one of the main speakers. Upon his arrival the whole audience rose to its feet shouting, "Dickinson! Dickinson!" The *Free Press* described the response to the chairman's proposal of "three cheers for Don M. Dickinson." "The enthusiasm was boundless. The ladies in the gallery were infected with the spirit, and fluttered their tiny handkerchiefs and smiled the rarest of smiles. The roof was almost raised by the volume of sound. Even the two handsome bouquets which stood on the little table in front of Mr. Dickinson quivered in sympathy."

In his speech Dickinson declared that he was speaking on "a plain subject, Grover Cleveland." For a time there were some politicians in Washington who could not understand this and considered Cleveland "a puzzle, an enigma," because they were accustomed "to the old condition of things." He illustrated his point by telling a story of an abnormal season of rainy weather in Zululand. The wet weather remained so long that the natives became accustomed to it. One day a light like a fire blazed up to the zenith and down to the horizon from a common center. The king, his court, and the wise men of the island all differed on what this meant. Some said it was the end of the world, others that the moon had fallen. Finally, "a plain old fellow from the backwoods came along and said, 'Why, friends, it is just going to clear off, and that what you see is the familiar, old-fashioned, God's sunshine and the glimmer of the blue vault of heaven.' "

Dickinson promised to return to Michigan during the closing days of the campaign. He kept his promise, and on October 27 he appeared before a crowd in Grand Rapids which the *Free Press* described as "the greatest political demonstration Grand Rapids has ever had." Describing Dickinson's reception, the Detroit newspaper elaborated: "Grand Rapids in its time has welcomed the little giant of Illinois, Stephen A. Douglas, and that favored leader of Democracy, Thomas A. Hendricks, but the reception that she gave those great leaders was dwarfed by the magnificent ovation that she gave today to the chivalric leader of the Northwestern Democracy, Don M. Dickinson. . . ."

On the eve of Election Day Dickinson made his last appearance of the campaign before a rally at White's Grand Opera House in Detroit. He spoke briefly at this meeting in defense of Cleveland's tariff policy. He averred that Cleveland realized "that a reduction of the tariff was the only method by which the prosperity of the working people could be maintained, and he relies upon the intelligence of the working people to understand this and support his efforts."

The next day the nation went to the polls, and Dickinson's beloved "Great Chief" went down to defeat though he had received a greater popular vote than his opponent. In spite of this, Dickinson refused to be downcast. He and Cleveland would suffer defeats later in which he would react as he did after the Greeley debacle. However, to this loss his response was anything but pessimistic. Several letters written soon after the 1888 election reveal this. Later in November he wrote, "We must simply reform the line and advance the standard. I have no doubt whatever of ultimate success because we are right." Later he expressed similar sentiments, saying, "I see no reason for dismay. The only thing to do is to reform and advance the standard. Remember the historical overthrow of Van Buren, and our magnificent triumph four years later; the disheartening defeat of 1880 and the election of Cleveland in 1884. There is no demoralization here." Dickinson lived to see his optimism rewarded by a smashing 1890 Democratic victory in Michigan and the successful campaign of Cleveland in 1892.

CHAPTER 5:

"YOU HAVE DONE GLORIOUSLY"

Midway through his term as postmaster general, Dickinson wrote that "there is nothing so bright to me in the future as the peace of unofficial life." After his term ended in March, 1889, he returned to his legal practice in Detroit. He seemed to be as busy as ever. Cleveland wrote to him in May, saying, "Of course, I was not surprised to learn that you were tugging away again in the harness, for it is your nature, and as long as you are willing there will be plenty to put on the load."

The following month he was "tugging away" as never before when he became involved in one of the most arduous legal cases of his entire career. In this case the Lake Superior Ship Canal, Railway, and Iron Company pitted itself against certain Upper Peninsula homesteaders seeking to prevent ejection from the land they occupied. Dickinson placed himself on the side of those families struggling to retain their homes.

The stage had been set when Cleveland signed the Forfeiture Act on March 2, 1889. Under this act land which had been given to

Michigan in 1856 to promote railroad construction within the state reverted to the federal government. Michigan had given this land to railroad companies, but tracks had not been extended into the area where the land had been granted, and so it was declared forfeited. At the same time the law specifically stated that the railroads involved might appeal to the courts.

Within a short time the Lake Superior Company did appeal for return of the land. The cause of the homesteaders looked bleak indeed when the federal court in Marquette ruled against the homesteaders and eviction proceedings began. Although Dickinson's efforts to obtain backing for a resolution favorable to the homesteaders failed in the state legislature, he won a significant victory when a United States Circuit Court overruled the previous decision, finding for the homesteaders and preventing their eviction.

While Dickinson was fighting this case, a Jackson newspaper reported that "in the cabins of the Homesteaders of the Upper Peninsula Mr. Dickinson's name is a household word, and he is revered by them as the one man who at all times and places has proved their true friend." That these sentiments correctly expressed their feelings became evident in 1891, after the Democrats had won control of the state's lower house. At that time a county created in the Upper Peninsula was named Dickinson County in honor of the man who had saved the homes of hundreds of homesteaders. Dickinson had refused financial compensation for the part that he played in this case; however, he was highly pleased with this move. He later wrote that the state legislature had honored him more by creating a new county and naming it after him than if it had elected him United States senator.

Although Dickinson was "rewarded" in 1891, the case that he fought for the homesteaders was not concluded until December 10, 1894. On that day the United States Supreme Court concurred in the United States Circuit Court's decision in favor of Dickinson and his clients, saying that any homesteader on the land on May 1, 1888, was "within the Act of March 2, 1889," and, therefore, "a bona fide claimant of a homestead."

Another significant legal case in which Dickinson became involved during these years was one in which he fought to save the law providing for a secret ballot in Michigan. The case testing this law involved the Detroit Common Council and Peter Rush, Detroit's Controller. The law sought to insure a secret ballot by prohibiting the outer attachment to any ballot or ticket of "any impression, device, color, or thing, designed or liable to distinguish such ballot or ticket from other legal ballots or tickets, whereby the same may be known or designated." No ticket was to be used at any state election unless furnished by the secretary of state. All ballots were to be of the same width and length. Booths were to be constructed where a voter could vote secretly, but Rush refused to advertise for bids to construct election booths as the law directed. Thus the Detroit Common Council sought a writ of mandamus to compel Rush to do so. Rush steadfastly refused. He claimed that the law was unconstitutional, that "the booths and railings will cost a large sum of money, and that no provision has been made by the law for paying the expense."

Dickinson and Alfred Russell represented the Common Council and argued that the law should be allowed to stand. The court ruled in favor of the law. In nullifying Rush's objections, the Michigan Supreme Court reviewed the evils that had sprung up causing the law to be enacted and finally declared: "The secrecy of the ballot is the great safeguard to the purity of elections. The vote by ballot implies secrecy." The court answered Rush's second objection by specifically stating: "It is of no consequence that expense must be incurred, and that the statute is silent upon the question of payment. Whenever an active duty is imposed upon municipalities, the duty imposed carries with it the obligation on the part of the municipality to perform the act, bear the expense, and provide for its payment."

A few days after the court had ruled, Dickinson said that this decision had made the Democrats more hopeful in Michigan. He went on to show that the Republicans had been against the law and had done what they could to defeat it. "I had the pleasure of appearing for our side in defense of the law," he said, "and you may be sure that I was much gratified at the outcome." He described Michigan as "a great State for 'boss' politics," with the Republicans usually in the majority and applying pressure on voters. "We have suffered a great deal from this in years past, and now that we consider that we have secured a preventive of it we expect that persons who have been kept from voting our ticket in former years through fear of losing the situations in which they have been employed will come to us this year."

Dickinson's involvement in cases such as these prevented him from playing an active role in the 1890 political campaign. One day prior to the election that year, Dickinson made his only major political appearance. That evening Detroit Democrats closed the campaign with a large political rally at which Dickinson presided. He assumed his position as leader for the evening by informing the audience that he had "some good news for you tonight and from it a lesson for Democrats tomorrow." The news that Dickinson had was a prediction by Tim Nester, a former Republican and former mayor of Marquette, that the Upper Peninsula was going to vote Democratic in 1890. The Upper Peninsula had traditionally been strongly Republican. Dickinson reminded his hearers that in 1884, in fact, the Democrats "went to the Straits" with a good majority, but that it had been overcome by the mining vote.

He concluded his remarks by denouncing the McKinley tariff, which had become a major issue in this campaign. Concerning the tariff he said: "The McKinley bill is with us always; at the table, at the bedside, in the kitchen, in the barn, in the churches and to the cemetery. Grover Cleveland, God preserve him till 1892, told the truth when he said the tariff was a tax."

On Election Day, the Michigan Democrats scored a tremendous victory over the Republicans—one that was unequalled since the Republican party had been formed. The Democratic candidate for governor, Edwin B. Winans, along with the remainder of the Democratic state ticket rode roughshod over the Republican opposition. In addition, the citizens of Michigan sent a Democratic majority to the state legislature.

The state Democrats, who had for years longed for the day that finally came in 1890, could not restrain the impulse to celebrate this victory with a gala victory rally in Detroit—a rally described as Fourth of July, Christmas, New Year's Day, St. Patrick's Day, German Day plus all other glorious days rolled into "one grand twenty-four hours." With victory certain, the event took place three days after the election. Before the evening meeting began, a bomb was ignited which also set the Democrats on fire for the evening. The *Free Press* described the scene. "With the bursting of this as a signal there arose a simultaneous flight of sky rockets, roman candles and other aerial pieces of pyrotechnics, until the whole sky in the vicinity of the rink was lighted."

Although Dickinson had been rather inactive in pre-election campaigning, Democrats still considered him an important leader. The *Evening News*, for example, in its edition on the day of the rally, commented, "There will also be present that Democratic cyclone, Don M. Dickinson, the leader of the state Democracy, whose soul is entirely impregnated with the idea of seeing Grover Cleveland justified for sticking to democratic principle by nominating him for President in 1892." One banner hanging over the stage the night of the rally read: "Hail to the Pride of Democracy, Don M. Dickinson."

Like Dickinson, Grover Cleveland retired from political life for a time after the 1888 defeat. He enjoyed private life and wrote: "You cannot imagine the relief which has come to me with the termination of my official term. There is a good deal yet which seems to result from the Presidency and the kindness of people in a social way which keeps me in remembrance of Washington life, but I feel that I am fast seeking the place I desire to reach—the place of a respectable private citizen." In September, 1889, he said, "Present personal interests are all against my appearing in the political field."

In spite of these utterances, Cleveland gradually became involved in national political affairs once again. In a letter to one of his former cabinet officers, Cleveland gave some inkling of his concern, even though he wanted his "discharge from public and political life." He explained: ". . . I am unable to lose sight of the possibility, or to forget that a contingency may arise, in which duty to my country and my party may require in me the elements of a popular candidacy." As time elapsed, it became more evident to Cleveland that such a contingency was emerging. As he viewed the actions of the Harrison administration, he became increasingly convinced that it was giving ground to those who sought the benefit of special privilege at the expense of the country's best interests. Democratic victories in 1890 also encouraged Cleveland. They seemed to vindicate his stand on the tariff, as even William McKinley, author of the prohibitive McKinley tariff, went down to defeat.

In spite of renewed interest, Cleveland gave no indication during 1891 that he would seek the presidential nomination. At times it seemed that he was not in the least concerned about his chances of renomination. A good example of this lack of concern was the famous "silver letter" to E. Ellery Anderson.[1] At that time many Democratic leaders were aligning themselves behind the movement for unlimited coinage of silver. In fact, in January, 1891, the Senate passed a bill favoring free coinage; many Democrats voted for it.

Even with this sentiment in his own party, Cleveland wrote to Anderson: "If we have developed an unexpected capacity for the assimilation of a largely increased volume of this currency, and even if we have demonstrated the usefulness of such an increase, these conditions fall far short of insuring us against disaster, if in the present situation we enter upon the dangerous and reckless experiment of free, unlimited, and independent silver coinage." There was an immediate outcry against this attack on free coinage. Daniel Lamont, a former private secretary of Cleveland, urged him to modify his stand so that the masses would not think him "the representative of the ultra anti-silver sentiment."[2]

During this time Dickinson hoped that Cleveland would allow his name to be presented for the presidential nomination. Even though Cleveland in 1891 spoke more freely on political matters than he had since retiring from the White House, his followers realized that he might step aside if a candidate acceptable to him came to the fore. However, in the year 1891, Governor David B. Hill of New York loomed as the most formidable challenger for the Democratic presidential nomination. Cleveland, along with Dickinson, was greatly opposed to this man's ambitions." Cleveland realized that Hill's nomination and election would be a severe blow to his chief principles of "sound money, tariff reform and civil service reform and departmental efficiency."

In January, 1892, the Democratic National Committee met to select the time and place for the national convention. A Cleveland sympathizer warned Dickinson that "a desperate effort will be made by the Tammany and Hill followers to bring the National Convention" to New York where the pro-Hill faction planned to "whoop it up" for Hill. Dickinson was urged to take action in Michigan in order to "head off a few hotheads who are captured with Hill's questionable audacity and present success."

At aoout the same time Dickinson wrote a letter to William Vilas, who also had served in Cleveland's cabinet, urging him to unite delegates from the West and South so that the convention would not be held in New York. Dickinson and Vilas were heartened when the National Committee chose Chicago as the site for the convention.

In a very short time the New York State Democratic Committee countered by scheduling a state convention at Albany on February 22 for the purpose of electing delegates to the national convention. The New York Democrats rarely held a state convention for this purpose as early as February. This "snap convention" would work against Cleveland's interests and for Hill's, because delegates to this convention would be chosen at caucus meetings of small town politicians allied with Hill. Few farmers from upstate would be able to attend because of inclement weather. It was hoped that an early New York convention would ignite Hill support throughout the country before anti-Hill Democrats could muster any strong movement for other candidates.[3]

Soon a cry of protest arose from all parts of the country. Many Democratic newspapers denounced the action of the New York Democrats. Supreme Court Justice Lamar wrote that the South had been aroused against the methods used to promote Hill's candidacy. In New York an "anti-snapper" movement advanced by those Democrats opposed to the tactics being employed gained momentum as anti-Hill Democrats formulated plans for a convention of "anti-snappers" at Syracuse.

In view of all of this, Dickinson, convinced that the time had come to begin Cleveland's bid, laid careful plans. He persuaded Cleveland to come to Ann Arbor and address students at the University of Michigan on the very day that the "snap convention" convened in New York. Dickinson believed that Cleveland would detail his ideals and principles and thus provide the keynote for his bid for a renomination.[4]

Cleveland accepted Dickinson's invitation and on February 22 did just what Dickinson had hoped in his Ann Arbor speech. Perhaps with the New York "snap convention" in mind, he advised the Michigan students: "Interest yourselves in public affairs as a duty of citizenship; but do not surrender your faith to those who discredit and debase politics by scoffing at sentiment and principle, and whose political activity consists in attempts to gain popular support by cunning devices and shrewd manipulation."

Several years later Dickinson wrote to Cleveland concerning his appearance in Ann Arbor. He told Cleveland that even before his speech interested citizens were already working for his renomination. Dickinson continued, "I remember how . . . after the winter of '91 we inveigled you out here to make that classic speech at the university, and then succeeded in getting the Ass.[ociated] Press to send out your speech and the account of all our doings here so as to be printed *ahead* of the proceedings of the 'Snap convention' held on the same day. It was the only mean trick I ever played on you, but you can't imagine how it strengthened the good fellows even then at work."

Dickinson realized that the account of the "snap convention" and Cleveland's speech would appear in the papers almost simultaneously. Thus, Cleveland supporters exercised special care in seeing that many newspapers and magazines were supplied with copies of the speech. The contrast between the actions of the pro-Hill faction in New York and the words of Cleveland in Ann Arbor convinced many Democrats that Cleveland should be their nominee in 1892. Instead of beginning a Hill boom, the New York convention had done Hill more harm than good.

After the Washington's Day address at Ann Arbor, Cleveland Democrats began to pressure the former President more and more. Edward S. Bragg, who earlier had expressed his admiration for Cleveland with the phrase, "We love him for the enemies he has made," warned of the dangers to the nation if the Democratic party failed to win in November. He requested that Cleveland reply affirmatively to the call of his country and party and announce his willingness to serve again.

A few days later Cleveland made it clear that he would run again.[5] In answer to Bragg's request he admitted reluctance: "If, in answering your question, I might only consider my personal desires and my individual ease and comfort, my response would be promptly made, and without the least reservation and difficulty." Nevertheless, Cleveland continued, if Bragg was right in his judgment, then "private and personal considerations" were made "entirely irrelevant." The letter closed with an expression of earnest concern for the success of the Democratic party.

In March, Hill made a tour of the Southern states hoping to gain support in an area where there was much opposition to Cleveland's money views. This tour proved to be a big disappointment to Hill and his followers. In Atlanta the rally for Hill was described as a "dismal failure." The editor of the *Chattanooga News* wrote to Cleveland: "Hill's canvassing jaunt has weakened beyond the shadow of a doubt even the little enthusiasm that has been aroused in the South. . . . His receptions were cool, in fact, almost chilly." Thomas Bayard, who had been Cleveland's secretary of state, wrote to Dickinson describing Hill's swing around the South: "From my point of view there never was a greater burlesque than the journeys of Mr. Hill in the role of President seeking." He wondered aloud whether Hill took "his countrymen for fools or worse." Bayard predicted that if his "own state of feeling" were indicative, "the machine will receive a dislocation at the next convention from which it will never recover." In May, Hill's chances were dealt a deathblow when Georgia, considered the strongest Hill state in the South, elected a pro-Cleveland delegation to the national convention.[6]

In January, Dickinson had expressed a wish that he "could help some" in the fight against Hill. He saw an excellent opportunity to do just that at the state convention. Dickinson scored a personal victory when his fellow Democrats elected him first delegate-at-large and chairman of the Michigan delegation to the national convention. After winning a unanimous vote, he spoke briefly to the assembled Democrats. He quickly indicated that he stood squarely behind Cleveland, saying that he "took great pride in the expression of myself as the first delegate-at-large from my state. But," he continued, "I quite appreciate that your hearts go out not so much for me upon this occasion as to the Great Chief, in whose official family I had the honor to serve."

A reading of the platform indicated complete victory for Cleveland and Dickinson in Michigan. Loud applause greeted the statement, "We, therefore, instruct our delegates to the national convention this day chosen to vote in that convention as one man for the nomination of Grover Cleveland to the presidency of the United States." Cleveland may well have breathed a "well done, Dickinson" when he received a telegram that same evening from Michigan Chairman Daniel Campau which summarized the action taken by the Michigan convention and declared, "In this action the delegation will express the exact sentiment of the Michigan Democracy which is for Cleveland and victory."

About a week after the Michigan state convention, Cleveland wrote Vilas, saying, "I cannot do less than say to you that some very warm friends think there should be a touching of elbows among those who think as you do on the Presidential question." When William C. Whitney, who had been one of Cleveland's principal aides, returned from Europe on May 18, plans were made for a strategy conference prior to the Democratic national convention. In planning this conference of influential Cleveland Democrats, Dickinson played a prominent role. He wrote to Vilas that it had been decided to hold a larger conference than first anticipated and "endeavor to reach a decision as to treatment of all matters likely to come up." Two days later Dickinson again wrote to Vilas reporting that Cleveland had suggested that the conference be held after the Republican convention in Minneapolis. He revealed that a proposal had been made that he, Dickinson, send out notices calling the conference, "but I thought it . . . better for W[hitney] to have done it and have so written him."

On the same day Dickinson wrote Whitney that he considered the ninth of June a "very good" date for the conference. At the same time he commented, "In names there are some omissions in the West and South." He advised that they be added, "as I think I have been in a way to know them during the past two months."

On June 9, twelve prominent Democrats from ten states met at Whitney's home on Fifty-seventh Street in New York. It was extremely inclement weather, but by 11:00 a.m. all those expected had arrived. At this significant conference detailed plans were made for the forthcoming convention, including the membership of important convention committees.

When the Democratic national convention convened in Chicago, the Cleveland forces chose Don Dickinson as their floor leader. Dickinson made his first major move on the second day of the convention when William F. Vilas read the first paragraph of the proposed platform. Vilas began: "The representatives of the Democratic Party of the United States in National Convention assembled to re-affirm their allegiance to the principles of the party as formulated by Jefferson and exemplified by the long and illustrious line of nine of his successors in Democratic leadership from Madison to Cleveland. . . ." When Vilas pronounced the name of Cleveland, it ignited one of the greatest demonstrations seen at a political convention.[7] Quickly Dickinson grasped the Cleveland banner of the Michigan delegation; while the band played the national anthem, he led a procession, "with the set face of a devotee, swinging the big censer high above his head while the crazed delegates gazed with eyes of longing and shouted with throats of brass at the swinging picture." For twenty minutes this continued, and it seemed that every delegate was on his feet except "the little squad from New York," seated near the Michigan delegation, "silent in the cheering mass." Dickinson and his Michigan delegation had propelled a wave that would roll Cleveland in on the first ballot.

After formal adoption of the platform, the convention set about the business of choosing a presidential nominee. When Arkansas yielded to New Jersey, Governor Leon Abbett of New Jersey nominated Cleveland. As soon as Abbett mentioned "Cleveland," the Michigan delegates touched off another demonstration. When Michigan's Cleveland banner passed New York's delegation, Daniel Sickles, a staunch supporter of Hill, pushed it aside. For a moment it appeared as if Dickinson and Sickles would physically clash, for, as Dickinson "expostulated," Sickles rose to his feet, "shook his crutch aloft, brandished his fist, and for a few minutes he assumed a belligerent attitude." The noisy uproar continued for fifteen minutes; Abbett then started again, and, on finishing, the *New York Times* correspondent reported, "... the convention went wild again. The white silk banner of the Michigan delegation was again hoisted by an enthusiastic Wolverine. Three men stood on chairs and waved it high until their arms ached. The band struck up a lively tune, and a thunderstorm which broke at the moment lent its music to the great uproar. Umbrellas were raised, hats were thrown in the air. Pandemonium reigned for another ten minutes."

The final maneuver on the part of the Tammany pro-Hill group came just before the first ballot. At that point Bourke Cockran of New York rose and requested that the convention be adjourned until the following morning, thus giving them more time to stem what seemed to be an irresistible Cleveland tide. Dickinson realized this and, as Cleveland's floor leader, sullenly shook his head. The convention followed Dickinson's lead. Cockran then made one of the best speeches heard at the convention. But it was not enough, and Cleveland won the nomination on the first ballot by a substantial majority.

As far as Dickinson was concerned, one battle had been won; but another lay ahead. A month after the convention he wrote his wife that he had "been all day with the Chief" and was still at the home of Whitney "getting some things in shape at his request." Cleveland considered it essential to have Whitney as the leader of "the committee to manage the national campaign." Thus, he urged those whom he thought most influential to write or speak to Whitney so that he would agree to perform this task. Those whom he requested to influence Whitney included his old friends Wilson S. Bissell, William Vilas, and Dickinson.

Dickinson was more than willing to help. However, Whitney resolutely refused to accept the chairmanship of the national committee. Dickinson sought to persuade others to write Whitney; but he would not accept, though he did not turn his back on the Democratic campaign. C. H. Jones of St. Louis wrote that Whitney had informed him "that he can accomplish more by being a free lance, unburdened with the details that fall upon the chairman, than by accepting the chairmanship." Whitney, though not accepting an official position, provided inestimable service all during the campaign and became the unofficial leader of it.

When Whitney refused the national chairmanship, there were fears on the part of some Democrats that Calvin Brice, national chairman in the unsuccessful 1888 campaign, might be selected again. One prominent Democrat from St. Louis asked for other possible choices for national chairman. He urged that Dickinson and "others of the party's wise counsellors" prevent mistakes "in this matter of officering of the National Committee." On July 18, Vilas wrote Dickinson telling him that an attempt was quietly being made "to retain the control of the Committee by Hill and Brice by keeping B. on as Chairman." Vilas confidently predicted, "We'll be able to defeat it." A struggle as to who should be national chairman never actually arose. Brice graciously withdrew, saying he would not accept the chairmanship again. Whitney nominated William F. Harrity of Pennsylvania, who was elected without opposition. Cleveland, apparently satisfied with the outcome, wrote to Whitney on July 29: "If things shape up as we expect, the campaign work will be in the hands of Harrity, Quincy, Dickinson and Whitney—four Cleveland men if there are any—and we shall have the prestige of a united party." About two weeks later the national committee chose Dickinson to head the Democratic National Campaign Committee.

Although Cleveland believed Whitney invaluable as a campaign leader, he disliked the fact that Whitney wished to go all-out in reconciling the Tammany group. He described Whitney as being as "true as steel" and one who worked day and night. "But his labor is altogether in the line of pacification and everything he does tends to persuading the men of Tammany Hall and those who belong to their gang to vote the Democratic ticket." Cleveland preferred to remain aloof and run without the support of Tammany Hall if necessary.

Finally, however, Whitney did induce Cleveland to meet with certain leaders of Tammany Hall in order to effect a policy of conciliation. Apparently Cleveland thought that Dickinson was more in accord with his thinking concerning Tammany Hall. Cleveland had good reason for so thinking since Dickinson had written him prior to the convention that Whitney was considering giving some influence to Arthur P. Gorman, which Dickinson felt "would probably be a beautiful compromise with shame." Gorman had been allied with the Tammany group, and Dickinson vowed that he was "out" if Whitney gave Gorman a place of influence.

Cleveland found a certain solace in confiding in Dickinson prior to the scheduled meeting with the Tammany leaders. On September 5, three days before the meeting, he wrote a confidential letter to Dickinson expressing his inner feelings. "I received a letter from Whitney a few days ago and had a talk with him Saturday. As a consequence of these combined incidents, I am thoroughly miserable and depressed and feel very much like doing a desperate thing. I am thinking very hard, and the thing that troubles me more than all others is the duty I owe to such good sincere friends as you. I feel as though I *must* see you."

In the last paragraph of this brief note Cleveland poured forth his reluctance to have anything to do with Tammany Hall, saying: "And, my dear fellow, if you do come, I beg you to come in a mood to believe that I am not always wrong and that I ought to be allowed to emerge from this campaign still deserving, in some degree at least, the respect of those whose good opinion I prize more than any office or honor, and still preserving to some extent my self-respect."

When Cleveland attended the Victoria Hotel conference three days later, Dickinson was at his side. The Tammany leaders present included Richard Croker, Edward Murphy, Jr., and William F. Sheehan. When Sheehan demanded recognition from the administration in the event that Cleveland should win, Cleveland simply replied, "No promises."[8] As the talk continued and Murphy "kept up a rumble of supporting growls in the background," Cleveland became angry and declared that he would rather withdraw from the race than make unethical concessions to Tammany Hall.

The story of Cleveland's re-election is a familiar one, with the nation seemingly intent on righting the wrong of 1888. This time Cleveland not only won a popular majority but a majority in the electoral college as well. Some Democratic leaders recognized that Dickinson had contributed significantly to the victory. Thomas Bayard complimented Dickinson, saying that he could imagine the joyous confusion at campaign headquarters "where in three months you have exhibited such force, tact, and good temper and vigilance in the great cause in which we are all enlisted. . . ." William G. Ewing, one of the prominent Democrats present at the Whitney conference on June 9 and a leader of Democratic forces in Illinois, wrote, "I have been near enough to the camp of the great commanders to know that to no one more than yourself is due credit of our wonderful triumph. Illinois is indeed a "rainbow" filled with hope and promise. Our people are grateful that you chased it." C. H. Jones, editor of the *St. Louis Republic*, sent a message saying, "You have done gloriously."

A short time after the election, Dickinson received a note from the President-elect. Cleveland, who should have felt as elated as any Democrat, confided to his close friend Don Dickinson, "I don't feel altogether comfortable, but there is no reason why I should bother you with my troubles. I only wish God would put it in my power to make known to the Democratic party what the last election means." The Great Chief rightly viewed the coming four years with some foreboding.

CHAPTER 6:

"YOU WILL HEAR NO MORE
OF DICKINSON"

After the 1892 Democratic victory Cleveland began the task of forming a cabinet. Although Dickinson preferred not to serve in any official capacity in the second Cleveland administration, Cleveland hoped to lure him into his official family once more and offered him "places in the Cabinet." Nonetheless, Dickinson refused a cabinet post, an opportunity to become Ambassador to Great Britain, and, shortly after Cleveland's inauguration, a position as one of the government's directors of the Union Pacific Railroad. In this last instance Dickinson wrote Cleveland: "I shall hold the fact that you named me for the place first, as you did, as one of the pleasantest, and most gratifying things that have come to me in my public life." He reiterated his stance of not wanting to accept "any place in the public service" and said he would feel "perfectly miserable if I merely attended to the duties in a perfunctory way. . . ."

During the weeks preceding the inauguration Dickinson conferred with Cleveland at different times. Cleveland appreciated his association with Dickinson, for he wrote Daniel Lamont during this time, "I am constantly wondering why there are not, within the circle of my life, more Lamonts and Dickinsons." When the President chose Dickinson's law partner, Henry T. Thurber, to be his private secretary, few doubted that Dickinson still had much influence with the Cleveland administration. This spot, held by Daniel Lamont during the first administration of Cleveland, was one of significant responsibility. The private secretary to the President answered much of the President's mail as well as meeting in person a great number of people who wanted to speak with the President. It was the responsibility of the private secretary diplomatically to steer many who wished to see the President to other government officials, offending as few as possible. He represented the President on some occasions when the Chief Executive could not be present. The private secretary served as one link between the President and legislative leaders.[1] Dickinson told Cleveland that his partner Henry Thurber possessed the qualities needed for this post and was "just the man for the position."

Four days after expressing a desire for more Dickinsons, Cleveland told Lamont that he had accepted Dickinson's man with thanks. Near the end of his second administration Cleveland revealed how highly pleased he had been with Henry Thurber. "As to Mr. Thurber, I can honestly say that of all things you have done for me, I regard your suggestion of his selection as private secretary the most useful and fortunate." He complimented Thurber, crediting him with having "plenty of ability, good discretion, a pure heart and conscience, unquestioned honesty, sufficient tact, and [as being] as loyal and devoted a helper as I have had about me."

Shortly after Cleveland's second inauguration, Dickinson wrote to Thurber, "Thousands here and all over the country say orally and write that they *know* that my relations with the President are such that if I say the word the desired appointment will follow and so on and so forth." He said "he was tired of it all" and longed for "complete and lasting oblivion after the seating of the President." When he wrote this letter, Dickinson seemed depressed, and the hopes that he expressed concerning oblivion and a complete retreat from the political battlefield were not fulfilled in the succeeding months, though he did not assume any official position during Cleveland's second term.

Early in April it seemed obvious to Dickinson that he could not sink into obscurity immediately, for he wrote Thurber that "there are many applications for letters of introduction from me to the President." Most of these requests Dickinson refused. However, he wrote that he had acceded in a few cases; but he directed Thurber not "to make any special provision as the ordinary method of treatment in the cases will do perfectly well. . . ." Besides this type of request, Dickinson received messages asking that he use his influence more directly. For instance, one Johnie Shea bluntly asked, "Please wire Mr. Thurber requesting my appointment. Am financially embarrassed."

Besides this kind of activity, he soon found that strife over federal patronage was to swirl about him once again. When Cleveland had assumed office eight years before, the Michigan Democratic party had been split over patronage. The Congressional delegation and Dickinson were constantly at odds. After Cleveland's success in 1892, the struggle began all over again.[2] In Michigan the struggle within the Democratic party for patronage presented a new alignment. In Cleveland's second term Dickinson found himself opposed by State Chairman Daniel J. Campau, who was allied with the four Michigan Democrats in the House.

The appointments already made and the fear that Dickinson might leave little for other Michigan Democratic leaders forced the Michigan congressmen and Campau to combine forces. In April, Campau met with the Michigan Democrats in Washington. At the conference one of the most important questions discussed was the part the congressmen and Campau should take in controlling appointments. They concluded that Campau's choices must prevail in districts having a Republican congressman. The meeting induced the *Evening News* to publish a cartoon of an office seeker before two idols—one was labelled Dickinson, the other Campau. The caption read, "Somewhat of a Dilemma," while in the office seeker's mouth were the words, "Which Boss Shall I Worship?"

The day after this conference Campau and the Democratic congressmen conferred with the President. Even though Cleveland was very cordial to them, the delegation was not as successful as they had hoped to be. Someone asked Cleveland if he planned to appoint men endorsed by Campau and the congressmen to federal jobs. One of those present admitted that it was a bit embarrassing when Cleveland responded by saying that he had no rules and wanted to get all the information he could regarding appointees. It was only a lull before the storm. On May 11, the *Evening News* placed the caption "Don M.'s Board" over a report that so-called district referees, who were local representatives of the administration—called "political henchmen of Don M. Dickinson" by the *Evening News*—had been appointed in the districts where Campau thought he would have influence as far as patronage went. All applications for such federal jobs as postmasterships had to pass through these men before the applicant would be given any consideration in Washington.

Campau was greatly disturbed by this turn of events.[3] He charged that "the direction of Michigan's political affairs" had been given over "to private persons holding no official station with the Democratic organization of Michigan." He criticized the appointments of these men and demanded that the names of these "referees" be made public "so that every candidate might have a hearing and a fair one."

Campau now immediately sought an interview with the President. After his visit with Cleveland, Campau left Washington for New York, making no comment concerning the talk he had had with the President. Although Dickinson continued to maintain "a sphynx-like silence," a friend of his, Louis E. Rowley of Lansing, explained the Dickinson side of the story. Rowley challenged Campau's declaration that he was speaking for the state committee rather than as an individual; Rowley knew that Campau had used this same ploy before. He accused Campau of "laboring under an exaggerated idea of his own place and his power." Rowley refuted the charge that Dickinson was a "private influence" holding no official relation with the Michigan state committee by pointing out that Dickinson had been National Campaign Committee Chairman and, therefore, could not serve in any official capacity in Michigan.

In spite of the Michigan wrangle, the Cleveland-Dickinson relationship remained unimpaired. A few days after Campau's conference with Cleveland, Dickinson spent two hours riding and conversing with Cleveland. When Josiah Quincy resigned as assistant secretary of state in October, Cleveland appointed a close friend of Dickinson, Edwin F. Uhl, to this post. The President had expressed his confidence in Dickinson once more. One Dickinson acquaintance, aware that this appointment had been made with Dickinson's approval, rather bluntly wrote to Dickinson, "You made, I know, no mistake in this case."

In Cleveland's second term, more discouraging and unhappy than the first, Dickinson sought to buoy his friend in the White House. In 1893, he assured the President that his faith had not diminished and encouraged Cleveland with words like these: "As the intelligent, unselfish and reflective people of the country sustain you now, so will there be universal endorsement later on. History will repeat itself with emphasis. Jefferson passed through it. Jackson's case was very much worse. And the clamorers and villifiers nearly broke Lincoln's heart. . . ."

The feud between the two factions in the Democratic party that seemingly had simmered down after the first months of the Cleveland administration livened in 1894 when the party formulated plans for the fall elections. Late in June the Democrats met in Grand Rapids in order to nominate a state ticket. Although both Dickinson and his rival Daniel Campau were present, Dickinson was in control. This was evident when Spencer Fisher was nominated for governor after Dickinson had convinced him to run. Campau only reluctantly acquiesced in the choice of Fisher.[4] The domination of the "referee" wing at the convention, plus the fact that Dickinson continued to be influential in getting federal appointments, prevented the stimulation of much good will between the two opposing sides.

Dickinson realized what this schism would do to the party's chances in November. His attempts to bring the two groups together prompted an *Evening News* report describing "an heroic effort" by Dickinson to make peace between the "referees" and "anti-referees." The Detroit newspaper reported that the faction opposed to Dickinson had been "sulking" since its "disastrous defeat" at the state nominating convention and that the supporters of the administration had promised more federal jobs to the "anti-referee soreheads in Michigan as an inducement to forgive and forget and whoop it up for Fisher and the rest of the state ticket."

The occasion for the "peace" parley was a gathering of Democratic leaders for the purpose of choosing campaign managers. The Dickinson faction sought to heal the wounds by supporting John Strong as chairman of the state committee. Strong was described as "Campau's old-time friend and political lieutenant."

However, this attempt to restore harmony failed when Strong refused to accept the chairmanship. Then, apparently in disgust, those opposed to the Campau wing selected Dickinson's law partner, Elliot G. Stevenson. The Democratic campaign would be run by the "referees." Fuel was further provided for this continuing feud when Dickinson and Stevenson decided that Levi Griffen should be supported as Democratic Congressional candidate from the First Congressional District. This came in the face of reports that some Democrats were opposed to the Griffen candidacy and favored William Maybury.[5] With the endorsement of Stevenson and Dickinson, Griffen had little trouble in gaining the nomination in what was described as the "quietest convention ever held in Detroit." The resignations of both Charles C. Casterlin and Samuel Robinson from the executive committee of the Democratic State Committee a few days later dashed all hopes of ending the rift. Both men were staunch Campau supporters. Members of the Dickinson wing believed that they had resigned in protest at Campau's request.

With the resignations of these two Democrats only a month prior to the election, any chance of a Democratic victory vanished. During this month the quarrel worsened as Tim Nester and Timothy Taraney, both leading Democrats, split with the Democratic gubernatorial nominee. Dickinson sought to rally Democratic forces by getting Vice President Adlai Stevenson to speak in Michigan shortly before the campaign ended. However, the damage had been done; without a unified Democratic party there was no chance of victory, for the Democrats were already in trouble as a result of the Panic of 1893.

On November 6, a day described as "a complete Waterloo for the Democracy," the Democratic party suffered a major defeat in Michigan. All twelve Congressional districts elected Republicans. The entire state Republican ticket led by Governor John T. Rich was victorious. The Democrats failed to elect a single state senator, while John Donovan of Bay City became the lone Democrat elected to the state's lower house.

The Democratic rift in Michigan was not the sole cause for this disaster. It was the GOP's year: Republicans were successful throughout the nation. Nonetheless, the fight between the followers of Dickinson and Campau was a factor in causing the defeat to be such a crushing one. Statistics revealed that many Democrats had not voted and that apathy or passive protest had reduced the Democratic vote. The *Free Press*, which had minimized party differences during the campaign, afterward quite candidly admitted that this friction was significant, in an editorial entitled "Democracy Beat Itself." The Detroit newspaper acknowledged that in Michigan there "were dissensions and seeking for revenges that had no proper place in a struggle where there was so much at stake. . . ."

In Washington, Democrats were also having their troubles. The issue of gold and silver money was a significant one throughout Grover Cleveland's second term. He began his second term in March, 1893, and almost immediately the nation was assailed by an economic panic. He thought it imperative that the Sherman Silver Purchase Act be repealed as one means of counteracting the Panic of 1893.

Thus, Cleveland called Congress into special session and requested that the silver-purchase act be repealed. Following the leadership of William L. Wilson, the House repealed this law by a comfortable margin. However, in the Senate the Silver Purchase Repeal Bill bogged down. In Cleveland's mind, members of his own party seemed opposed to the best interests of the country. Cleveland frankly admitted to Dickinson, "I am very much depressed. I feel that I am looking full in the face a loss of popular trust in the Democratic party which means its relegation to the rear again for many years if not its disruption." Cleveland remarked that one phrase in a letter Dickinson had written to him a short time before "touches me deeply." He referred to Dickinson's statement that there were those who could help, but "pass by on the other side." Perhaps because there seemed to be so many of this kind, Cleveland concluded with, "I wish there were about twenty Dickinsons in the country."

Cleveland promised Dickinson that the struggle would continue "until no further fight can be made." He refused to compromise, and on October 30 the Senate passed the Silver Purchase Repeal Act. There were many who commended Cleveland for his persistence. Dickinson, as happy as Cleveland himself over this victory, commented, "Hail to the Chief who in triumph advances."

After the 1894 midterm election, the currency issue began to divide Michigan Democrats. Less than a month after the November election, George P. Hummer, a free silver Democrat from Holland and no friend of Cleveland, called a meeting in Detroit of Democratic leaders thought to be in favor of free silver. At the meeting there was sentiment expressed that a new independent silver party be formed outside the Democratic framework. However, most of those present ignored it and felt that it would be better to reorganize the party from within. Although ostensibly not a meeting of anti-Dickinson Democrats, it was evident that this group would be such a meeting when one delegate indicated that the proposed movement was not against any of the individual party leaders unless "those leaders put themselves in an attitude of hostility to silver." To most Michigan Democrats it became increasingly clear that Dickinson stood with Cleveland on the silver issue.

A "grand state round-up of 'no boss' free silver men" scheduled for December gave further impetus to this movement. At the parley in Lansing the participants passed resolutions favoring the free coinage of silver and requesting organization of the party in a manner favorable to free silver. Lines were drawn for a battle involving a major issue, not just the fortunes of a comparatively small number of office seekers.

As troubles continued to beset the Cleveland administration, the President found consolation in confiding his feelings to trusted and close friends. Shortly after his birthday Cleveland expressed gratitude to Dickinson for remembering the day. The President intimated that the messages from his friends were especially gratifying at this time, partially because "I have had some occasion to feel unusually forlorn during the last year." Three days later Dickinson assured the President that history would prove the second term of Cleveland to be the most difficult period in which a President ever had to lead the country. He added that history would also show "that the Chief, standing above, was great in his place, equal to every occasion, a patriot always, and in himself the bulwark that turned back the flood of destruction."

By early 1896, it became increasingly clear that the silver issue would be the primary one throughout that year's political campaign. Fully aware of this, Cleveland was convinced that if the free silver faction gained control of his party, the Democrats would suffer a setback similar to the one that had been dealt them by the party's stand on slavery. With this in mind Cleveland sought to reanimate the Democratic leaders whom he knew might have a chance of stemming the free silver tide.

During the early months of 1896, Cleveland corresponded with Dickinson frequently. In almost every case he sought to impress upon Dickinson the seriousness of the situation and the need for leadership on the part of those who could save the party from going down the wrong road. In February, he wrote a letter intimating that Dickinson should actively enter the 1896 campaign.

About a month later Cleveland wrote a note thanking Dickinson for a painting of a duck hunter. Rather morosely he reflected, "It is a very relieving picture to look at and every time my eye falls on it in these dreadfully dark and trying days, I say to myself, 'I wish I was in that old fellow's place.' " The President revealed that he looked forward with anticipation to the adjournment of Congress and the end of his term. At the same time he was concerned about the future of the Democratic party, saying, "I am positive there is but one chance for future Democratic successes—a perfect and unequivocal sound money platform at Chicago." Less than a week later the President rather diplomatically sought Dickinson's support when he asked, "Can there not be a majority at hand of sound-money delegates sent from Michigan to Chicago?"

As the days and weeks progressed and as he read letters sent to him by the President, Dickinson slowly weakened. He wrote to his wife in March that he had received frequent letters from the Chief, at the same time commenting, "I may get into the fight after all, as he has given the trumpet call. I will try to keep out, but his request you know is a great power with me. . . ." Three days after he had written to his wife, Dickinson made his decision. He informed Cleveland, "Regarding Michigan I will face about and do my best."

Dickinson reminded Cleveland that after the 1892 campaign, from which he had emerged "grey and bald and old," he had "determined to get out and stay out for good and all." Dickinson's boundless affection and respect for Cleveland had moved him to become a crusader for Cleveland and his cause once more. He expressed his motives: "I did, and do want a humble place in the political history of the time, and that is to have it said that I never failed or faltered in loyalty to the President, elected, defeated, and elected, who was the only Democrat who could have been elected since the war, and who stood for and filled the type of all that was good in the Democratic party. . . ." He promised to "do my part, which shall be my best." There would be many obstacles. "But," said Dickinson, the political soldier, "we will buckle to and do our duty from now on as you see it."

Dickinson's first opportunity came at the Democratic state convention scheduled for April 29. National Democratic leaders deemed Michigan's convention extremely important; they speculated that the action taken by the Michigan Democrats would give some indication regarding the stand of the midwestern states on the currency issue. Thus, when the convention opened in Detroit, Democratic leaders throughout the nation eagerly awaited the outcome.

Four days before the state convention, Wayne County Democrats came out in support of Dickinson. They expressed full approval "of his course as leader of the Democracy of Michigan." Perhaps more important to Dickinson was the defeat of a resolution favoring free silver and the choice of a delegation solidly in favor of the administration's stand on sound money.

Although he had been highly successful in throttling the silver faction at the Wayne County convention, Dickinson knew that the big test would come at the state convention. When Democratic leaders from all over the state of Michigan began to congregate on the eve of the convention, feelings ran high. The day before the convention the *Evening News* depicted Dickinson and George P. Hummer, a leader of the free silver forces, running after a ball hit into the air labelled "Dem Convention." Above the cartoon the caption read, "A Collision Inevitable." When the rumor spread that sound-money Democrats sought a compromise, Hummer, as well as others opposed to the gold Democrats, vowed that it was "Sixteen to one or bust and no quarter." This belligerent attitude, reported the *Evening News*, "is why every train coming into Detroit last night brought in parties of silver and anti-silver braves, all in full war paint and carrying scalping knives."

Dickinson spent most of his time on the day prior to the convention around the anti-silver headquarters. When asked whether he thought the free silver Democrats had enough votes to control the convention, he replied, "We do not think so." The free silver forces had claimed a sizeable majority, but Dickinson said it reminded him of a story about some frogs. He related a tale about a man who came to a hotel keeper seeking to make a sale of a carload of frogs. The hotel keeper could not handle that amount, nor even a wagon load, but he did finally agree to buy a bushel of frogs. "In due time," continued Dickinson, "the man came around with a pillow case in his hand and turning it over he dumped just fourteen frogs out on the floor." When the hotel keeper reminded him that he had first spoken of bringing in a carload and had actually brought much less than a bushel, he explained, "Well, you see it was this way. When I came across that swamp the frogs made so much noise that I thought there were 14,000,000 of them, but when I got down to catching them, that was all I could find."

The following day Dickinson performed what was termed a "miracle."[6] The convention endorsed the Cleveland administration, and Michigan Democrats chose a majority of pro-Cleveland delegates out of a twenty-eight-man delegation. The twenty-eight were instructed to vote as a unit on all questions coming before the national convention. The so-called miracle had not been performed without much hard work by Dickinson and Elliot Stevenson, chairman of the State Central Committee. The free silver leaders had not made certain that all free silver delegates would be present, while Dickinson and Stevenson had appointed committees throughout the state to make sure that pro-administration representatives would be at the state convention. As a result, most delegates who sympathized with Cleveland were there, whereas about one-third of the free silver delegates did not attend the convention. In Detroit, a committee of fifty "well-drilled" politicians who favored Dickinson and Cleveland met and spoke with all incoming delegates. They were careful not to antagonize those favoring free silver by diametrically opposing their views, but they did raise doubts by asking whether Michigan Democrats could afford to antagonize the administration.

The free silver forces also hurt themselves. They appeared over-confident. The *Grand Rapids Democrat* believed that the "impolite attack" on the President had driven many delegates to support the President and, therefore, was the principal cause of defeat.

Two days after the convention Cleveland expressed his gratitude. "I steal a moment from working hours to write this, because I feel I cannot longer refrain from expressing my thanks, as a citizen and a Democrat, to you and those who worked with you for the splendid achievement . . . in Michigan." The jubilant President expressed his appreciation and averred "how much prouder than ever" he was of Dickinson's friendship. Secretary of the Treasury John Carlisle wrote in a similar vein congratulating Dickinson "on your magnificent victory." He predicted that the fight for sound money would be "more vigorous and determined than ever."

The April 30 edition of the *New York Herald* entitled the story of the Michigan Democratic convention "Don M. Dickinson Wins" and *The New York Sun* published a poem entitled "The Destruction of Michigan Silverites."

> Don Dickinson came down like a wolf on the fold,
> His cohorts all gleaming with sound-money gold,
> And the sheen of their votes was like stars on the sea,
> That is, as near yellow as starlight can be.
>
> Like the leaves of the forest when summer is green,
> His host with their banners in Detroit were seen;
> Like the leaves of the forest when autumn hath blown,
> Were the silverites after the result was made known.
>
> For the voters of Don spread their wings on the blest,
> And flapped in the face of the foe as they passed;
> And the eyes of the silverites waxed deadly and chill,
> And their nerve but once heaved, and forever was still.
>
> And there lay one leader; a slug in the neck
> Had left him in such a condition of wreck
> That he couldn't have told you, with any regard
> For the truth, what it was that had hit him so hard.
>
> And there lay another, distorted, and pale,
> With a bug in his ear and a twist in his tail;
> And the others were scattered around on the floor,
> With Don and his cohorts still hunting for more.
>
> There was weeping and wailing and gnashing of teeth,
> And Don sitting down on the proud silver wreath,
> And the sun, which had shone with a bright silver light,
> Grew golden and shone like the moonshine at night.
>
> For the silverites sadly the battle bewail,
> For their idols are smashed in the temple of Baal;
> And some of them swear that the party shall split,
> While the others, grown wiser, respond to them, "Nit."

During the weeks preceding the national convention, Dickinson and Cleveland were in constant contact. Late in May Dickinson informed Cleveland of a letter he had written to National Chairman William F. Harrity suggesting that committees of "substantial men" be formed to act as pressure groups upon delegations to the national convention. Dickinson was convinced that "substantial men of character and standing, having a stake in the right decision of public questions," would be extremely influential in swaying the average delegate. "With proper organization of this kind," Dickinson concluded, "we could turn even a minority with a firm two-thirds."

Cleveland "so fully approved" of Dickinson's suggestion that he began to "agitate the subject in question where I thought it would effect the best results." Cleveland admitted disappointment in the reaction of some who seemed already willing to concede the convention and presidential nomination to the forces of free silver. "Michigan seems to be the only State where work was needed and forthcoming," Cleveland commented.

As the time for the Democratic showdown approached, Dickinson feverishly sought to reinvigorate the pro-Cleveland supporters. Cleveland wrote Dickinson for advice concerning one senator who "seemed indifferent" as to whether or not he should attend the Democratic convention. "What do you want to do about him?" asked Cleveland. The President was fully cognizant of Dickinson's efforts and added that the party could be saved with a "few more Dickinsons." At the same time Cleveland made mention of William Whitney, the man many thought could do much to save the administration's cause at the national convention if he became determined to do so. However, Cleveland said he had "no idea how Whitney will be 'hitched up' and with whom if he goes."

The very day that this letter was written Whitney decided to cancel a proposed trip to Europe and help lead the sound-money forces at the Chicago convention.[7] Dickinson, perhaps remembering Whitney's conciliatory gestures toward Tammany Hall in 1892, was suspicious of Whitney's motives. Dickinson charged that the national committee had a majority of ten in favor of sound money, but that the efforts of the gold Democrats were "about paralyzed" by "the attempted reincarnation of the Bunco-Steerer by Mr. Whitney." The "Bunco-Steerer" appeared to be Calvin Brice of Ohio or Arthur P. Gorman of Maryland, both of whom Dickinson bitterly opposed. In fact, he went so far as to assert that he would rather support Hill than the man he accused Whitney of promoting. In Dickinson's mind, Hill at least worked openly against Cleveland while "the other man is an assassin."

Dickinson was wrong in mistrusting Whitney. Cleveland was happy to have Whitney again so actively engaged on his side.[8] Dickinson himself tacitly admitted his misjudgment of Whitney's motives when he boarded a special train of eastern sound-money leaders sponsored by Whitney. This Chicago-bound train was used to plan the strategy that would be employed in an effort to nominate William E. Russell, the leader of sound-money forces in New England, for the presidency. Upon arriving in Chicago, Whitney, hoping to duplicate his success of 1892, arranged a conference of sound-money leaders. Although the gold Democrats seemed to be outnumbered, there was no indication that they were ready to concede to their opponents. Dickinson expressed the sentiment of the anti-silver group when he was asked what the sound-money backers hoped to accomplish. He responded by saying that they proposed to stand together and fight to the finish.

During the days immediately preceding the convention, the disgruntled silverites from Michigan began a movement to disqualify a number of the gold Democrats in the Michigan delegation. These Michigan insurgents sought to rally support among Democrats who were in sympathy with their cause. From comments recorded, it appears that there were delegates who were fully as eager to fell Dickinson as to promote the cause of silver.

The *Evening News* reported that Dickinson drew "first blood" before the convention opened. The basis for this report was the fact that the national committee agreed that the Michigan delegation as it had been chosen should be allowed to sit at least until the convention was permanently organized. Also, in a caucus held by the Michigan delegation the night prior to the opening of the convention, Elliot Stevenson had been chosen to be national committeeman over Daniel Campau by sixteen votes to eleven.

On July 7, National Chairman Harrity called the convention to order. The first major test came almost immediately in the election of a temporary chairman. Although David Hill, a gold Democrat, had been proposed by the national committee, he was rejected in favor of Senator John W. Daniel of Virginia by a vote of 556 to 349. The tide that would eventually sweep in William Jennings Bryan now began to flow rapidly. On the second day of the convention the silver-controlled committee on credentials unseated four gold Democrats from Michigan and replaced them with silverites. Since Michigan was bound by the unit rule, the Michigan delegation of twenty-eight now fell into the ranks of the silver forces. At the same time the entire Nebraska gold delegation was expelled, and sixteen silverites headed by Bryan took their places.

On Thursday, Senator James K. Jones presented the majority platform. The platform upheld free silver, and the administration of Cleveland was so vehemently assailed that even many of the silver delegates seemed stunned. It was now a foregone conclusion that some Democrat favoring free silver would win the presidential nomination. On Friday, July 10, the Democrats nominated Bryan and in so doing ended the Cleveland era.

Even before the Democratic national convention had adjourned, there was talk of a bolt by the gold Democrats. During July and August this movement grew, as midwesterners William Vilas of Wisconsin, John M. Palmer of Illinois, and Don Dickinson of Michigan led the way.[9] On August 7, a call was issued for a convention to be held in Indianapolis in September. When the convention met, the National Democratic party was born, endorsing sound money and low tariffs. John M. Palmer was nominated for President.

That Dickinson favored the new National Democratic party is evidenced by a letter from Abram S. Hewitt to Dickinson informing him that Hewitt had raised $32,500 "to supplement an equal amount to be raised by you for the expenses to be incurred in Michigan, Indiana, and Kentucky." The goal of the splinter group was evident when Hewitt concluded, "I trust that you will be able to secure the remainder of the money imperatively needed to insure the defeat of Bryan." Although on Election Day the party polled only 135,000 votes, it diverted votes in enough states so that McKinley was able to capture them, and thus it did "insure the defeat of Bryan" as Hewitt had wished.[10]

Before 1896, Dickinson's enemies had often predicted his demise, but he had always been able to bounce back as strongly as ever. For many years he had been the most powerful and influential figure in the Michigan Democratic party. At the April 29 Michigan Democratic convention he had seemed invincible: the convention backed the administration, the gold standard, and Don Dickinson, too. But the end of Dickinson's power and influence in his party came quickly. When four Michigan gold bug delegates were expelled in favor of the silverites at the national convention, when the Cleveland administration was repudiated, and finally when, as a result, those same Democrats, including Dickinson, bolted the party, the latter was finished as a Democratic leader. When it was later suggested that the party be reorganized along the lines that Cleveland would have liked, ponderous old Ollie James of Kentucky summarized the feelings of many Democrats when he declared, "Judas Iscariot would have had as much right to have been clambering over the hill of Calvary after his Master's Crucifixion attempting to reorganize the believers in Christianity as Grover Cleveland, John Carlisle or Don Dickinson have to rush forth to reorganize the party they betrayed." In Michigan Timothy Taraney buried Dickinson—this time for good—saying, "You will hear no more of Dickinson in Michigan Democratic politics."

CHAPTER 7:

"A MEMORY...CHERISHED AND REVERED...BY THE PEOPLE OF HIS NATION"

Dickinson lost the prestige he had once enjoyed within the Democratic party by refusing to support his party's nominee in 1896. After that campaign Democrats would never again give him the recognition which was his for some twenty years. Never again would he attend party conventions and hear shouts of acclaim at the mention of his name. After 1896 he was through politically. However, he continued to have an avid interest in politics. Even though he no longer had political power and influence, Dickinson did make some contributions to the nation. One contribution was in the matter of the Bering Sea claims. Cleveland had named Dickinson Chief Counsel for the United States before the Bering Sea Claims Commission just prior to the Democratic national convention in 1896.

The Bering Sea Claims Commission had been created as a result of the findings of the Paris Seal Fisheries Tribunal. The Paris court decided that the United States owed Canadian sealers compensation for illegally seizing British and Canadian vessels in the Bering Sea from 1886 to 1892. This tribunal stated that "the carrying out of the Regulations determined upon by the Tribunal of Arbitration, should be assumed by a system of stipulations and measures to be enacted by the two Powers. . . ."[1] On February 8, 1896, the United States and Great Britain concluded an agreement calling for the appointment of two commissioners, one from the United States and the other from Britain, to deal with the matter. The United States appointed William L. Putnam, and the British named George E. King. If these two commissioners would be able to agree, they would determine the claims for damages; if they would not be able to agree, the case would be referred to a mutually acceptable umpire.

In November, 1896, hearings began in Victoria, British Columbia amid much cordiality. Dickinson referred to the British delegation as "delightful fellows," and on Thanksgiving Day the British attorneys were hosts at a dinner for the Americans. Dickinson thoroughly enjoyed this assignment. He described the opposing counselors as "able men, fighting with credit for their Government and if any one could catch the old man napping, they would. . . . All the same, my old head never was working in better shape."

The commission spent more than two months hearing testimony and examining witnesses. In February, 1897, it adjourned. The commission met a single time at Montreal on June 16 and then adjourned again until August 25, when the oral arguments were scheduled to begin.

At that time Dickinson began his argument by saying, "I know no more fitting words to open the discussion than the words used by her Majesty's counsel, 'Peace hath its victories no less renowned than war.' " He pointed out that the entire principle of arbitration was on trial. "Peace is the desire of the world, but you cannot pluck peace as a child plucks fruit from the tree." The spirit that Dickinson displayed in his opening remarks prevailed throughout the session. Press comments indicate that Dickinson presented the American case well, even though the commission eventually awarded Great Britain $473,151.26. The most significant contribution made by the commission and the American and British attorneys was the harmonious way in which the proceedings were conducted. Dickinson's conduct as senior American counsel went far toward making this arbitration successful.

Probably a letter from Grover Cleveland regarding his efforts pleased Dickinson more than anything else. His old friend wrote, "I have not been entirely ignorant of the faithfulness and zeal of your service and I need not tell you how proud and gratified I have been when I have received information of your conduct." The former President thanked him heartily "for the complete manner in which you have vindicated the choice of counsel by the last Administration."

After 1896, Cleveland and Dickinson both remained interested in politics, though both had retired from the political wars. Cleveland enjoyed receiving correspondence from Dickinson, for he wrote to Dickinson in 1898 that he had not heard from him in a long time and had decided "to make an epistolary attack upon you, hoping thereby to hear something directly from you. . . ." He admitted that although "public affairs and politics have gained such a start of me that I despair catching up with the procession," he still took immense interest in these activities. Their correspondence indicates that they fervently hoped that the party would return to the principles for which Cleveland had stood. A year after the 1896 election Cleveland considered himself a political outcast, but at the same time he saw "that matters are brewing that may bring decent men into activity again."

During McKinley's first term Cleveland became perturbed with the growing spirit of imperialism within the United States. Concerning this menace he wrote Dickinson, "It would be strange, I think, if the sober second thought and patriotic common sense of our countrymen did not assert themselves in time to avoid disaster. . . ." At the same time he was disappointed with Democratic leadership. Writing to Dickinson about a year later, he commented, "Don't you in these days sometimes pinch yourself to see if you are awake when you contemplate so-called Democratic management?"

When the Democrats again nominated Bryan in 1900, sound-money Democrats such as Dickinson, John Carlisle, and Richard Olney again had to decide whether or not to support the Democratic ticket. For many the decision was difficult, because Democrats like Cleveland agreed with Bryan's anti-imperialistic stance but disagreed with him on the free coinage of silver.

Although such men as Carlisle and Olney supported Bryan as the lesser of two evils, in 1900 both Dickinson and Cleveland refused to do so. During the campaign many Bryanites were eager to gain Cleveland's endorsement and began to draw erroneous conclusions that Cleveland supported Bryan because both he and Bryan viewed American imperialism with some skepticism.[2] Cleveland, however, made it clear to Dickinson that he had no intention of doing this. The former President wrote that he was nearly "pestered to death" with appeals to back Bryan and for advice as to which candidate should be supported. Apparently a large majority of his correspondents hoped Cleveland would support Bryan, for he wrote that he could not do "what the large majority desires." On the other hand, Cleveland showed no inclination to support McKinleyism "affirmatively," and therefore he said, "I have thought I might satisfy my conscience and avoid the accusation of open and pronounced ingratitude by keeping silence."

Cleveland maintained this position throughout the campaign. Dickinson also remained aloof until October. Some supposed that gold Democrats like Dickinson would support Bryan if the sixteen-to-one plank were eliminated from the platform. However, as the campaign wore on, there seemed to be less likelihood of this.

In a letter to Theodore Roosevelt early in October Dickinson hinted that he would support McKinley and Roosevelt. Before endorsing the Republican ticket, Dickinson needed a more detailed explanation of a charge made by Bryan accusing the Republican legislature of failing to curb the ice trust in New York. The very next day Roosevelt replied. He thanked Dickinson for his letter and explained in detail his dealings with the ice trust. Roosevelt charged the Bryan leaders with hypocrisy: "In the Tammany state convention in New York they actually denounced the ice trust in their political capacity while in their private capacity they were stockholders in it and through their counsel were doing everything to prevent its dissolution by the attorney-general."

On October 23, the *Detroit Free Press* headlined its top news story, "Stand of a Gold Democrat." This story contained a formal statement by Donald M. Dickinson explaining why he was planning to vote for McKinley. He revealed that he had not planned to vote for Bryan since the convention at Kansas City had nominated him. However, said Dickinson, "I hoped for a time that I might with clear conscience stay away from the polls." Recent speeches by Bryan had changed all this, and Dickinson now admitted that he was forced to vote against Bryan. He avowed that he was still a Democrat and could never be a Republican. Nevertheless, Dickinson stated that he scarcely recognized "a vestige of Democratic principle" in the Democratic platform. Dickinson charged Bryan with preaching the gospel of hate by appealing "to the envious, the discontented, the improvident, the incompetent and the unworthy idle." He pointed out that the words of the old Biblical prophet Samuel concerning David aptly described Bryan and his followers—"And everyone that was in distress, and everyone that was in debt, and everyone that was discontented gathered themselves unto him, and he became a captain over them."

In September, Dickinson wrote to Cleveland admitting it was "a thousand fold harder passively to aid McKinleyism than it was in '96, but the alternative is 'a deep pit, and he that falls therein is abhorred of the Lord.' " The aid of which Dickinson spoke was passive largely because Dickinson did no campaigning, except for one speech delivered at a rally of sound-money Democrats late in October.

Even though there was a lack of wholehearted support, the Republicans were glad that Democrats such as Cleveland and Dickinson maintained the attitudes that they did. After a Republican victory more decisive than that of 1896, Theodore Roosevelt wrote to Cleveland: "I think now we have definitely won out on the free-silver business and therefore I think you are entitled to thanks and congratulations." In a similar vein, Roosevelt wrote to Dickinson:

> My dear Mr. Dickinson: I feel a very keen sense of gratitude to you personally, and I hope I need not say to you how deeply I feel the debt due to the Democrats who stood for sound money and civic honesty; and the responsibility which I certainly feel to them and which I hope and believe my whole party feels. In this State as Governor I think that relative to their numbers I have made rather more appointments from among gold Democrats than from among the Republicans, and from what I know they regard them as of infinitely more consequence. I think I have handled the Governorship along the lines they believe in. I can do very little, my dear sir, but what I can do I shall most earnestly try to do in a way that will not make you regret your part in the late election.[3]

Vice President Roosevelt was correct in assuming that he could do little to reward Dickinson while he was Vice President. However, in 1901, when he became President after the assassination of McKinley, he honored Dickinson by naming him to an arbitration tribunal which was directed to settle a dispute between the United States and San Salvador. Dickinson deeply appreciated this recognition. He later wrote, "As to my positions under the National Government, I esteem my professional positions in international matters, both as counsel for the United States and as arbitrator, more highly than any mere political place."

Although Dickinson was happy again in his legal practice, he could never lose the interest that he had in politics and the Democratic party. His optimism rose as the country's appreciation for Cleveland increased after 1900.[4] In the spring of 1903, Dickinson told Cleveland that in the South he had "invariably" heard Bryan's name "received with a *cuss*." He realized that Cleveland's name was again coming to the fore, commenting, "You know perfectly well all over this country men are using your name quietly." This, said Dickinson, explained the hysterics of Bryan, "the ass from Nebraska," as he enjoyed calling him.

In 1903, with Cleveland again rising in public esteem, talk began to circulate that he would run for President in 1904. Cleveland had no intention of doing this. When he was invited to attend the opening of the Louisiana Purchase Exposition at St. Louis on April 30, he requested Dickinson's advice as to whether he should publicize his determination not to run again. Although Dickinson was thoroughly convinced that Cleveland should not contend for the presidency again, he persuaded the latter to say nothing at the time concerning his intentions. Dickinson argued that this would drive friends of Cleveland into the arms of the Republicans.[5]

In 1904, Cleveland believed that either Richard Olney or Senator George Gray of Delaware would be the best Democratic presidential candidate. Other than Cleveland, Dickinson thought that Judson Harmon of Ohio would be the strongest Democratic nominee. Dickinson admired Harmon, who was also a lawyer, for his successes in battling trusts and monopolies. "Harmon would grow with every day of the canvass, and with every addition to the knowledge of him," concluded Dickinson. "Take him with a Southern man like Fitzhugh Lee, and you have an unassailable ticket."

Prior to the Democratic convention, Dickinson wrote to Harmon himself advising Harmon on certain procedures that he should follow. Said Dickinson, "I think everything is going right, but the agitation must be set afoot by your friends, wherever you can put it across the border into the South and elsewhere." Dickinson expressed confidence that Michigan would support Harmon and revealed that he was writing to Wisconsin, "which has a favorite and a mighty weak son."

At the same time Dickinson wrote to Jacob M. Dickinson, a Democratic leader in Chicago. In this note he included a strong endorsement of Harmon. It appeared to Dickinson that there really was no outstanding Democrat and that many delegates would come to the St. Louis convention "as wandering sheep." In the South, Dickinson stated, "there is less and less muscle and earnestness" in the movement to nominate Judge Alton B. Parker.[6] He requested that Jacob Dickinson have a "downright strong talk" with the leader of the Illinois delegation to the convention. Dickinson's lack of influence in the Democratic party was well illustrated, however, when Harmon's name was scarcely mentioned during the days preceding the convention. Although Dickinson had expressed optimism regarding Harmon support among Michigan Democrats, the Michigan delegation to the national convention cast all twenty-eight of its votes for Judge Parker, who received the nomination on the first ballot.

Although Cleveland had expressed a preference for his former cabinet member Richard Olney or Senator George Gray of Delaware, whom he had wanted to include in his cabinet, the former President was not dissatisfied with the nomination of Parker. He wrote Parker soon after his nomination, "Our best campaign material just now is—YOU." He was especially happy with Parker's strong statement in favor of the gold standard.

Dickinson was not as pleased as Cleveland was. Three months before the convention Dickinson had charged that Parker had aided David B. Hill in his successful drive to be elected Democratic governor of New York in 1888, while at the same time doing as little as possible to aid the national ticket headed by Cleveland. The motive behind this, Dickinson believed, was to prove that a presidential candidate could not be elected without New York's electoral votes. The election of Hill and the defeat of the national ticket in New York would have placed Hill in a favorable position as far as the 1892 presidential race was concerned. "These facts show why I do not favor Parker." Although Dickinson almost immediately apologized for this statement, saying that it was incorrect, he never supported Parker in the same way that Cleveland did.

McKinley and Roosevelt won easily in 1900. When McKinley was fatally wounded less than a year after his victory, Roosevelt became President. As time went on Dickinson's admiration for Roosevelt grew. In 1908, he wrote a letter to President Roosevelt urging him to run again. He explained that he had ascertained "the sentiment of our people of both parties." He argued that it would not actually be considered a third term, since Roosevelt had only been elected to the presidency once. He praised the President "as the most fearless

77

of all Presidents in preserving and protecting all the people against wrong, theft, and oppression."

Although Roosevelt did not follow Dickinson's advice in 1908, Dickinson continued to respect him. Even though he held Woodrow Wilson in high esteem, Dickinson supported Roosevelt again in 1912. Shortly before illness disabled him, Dickinson wrote to Roosevelt:

> I beg to tender you my heartfelt sympathy and expression of my unfaltering belief in your lofty aspirations and acts for the benefit of this Republic. You have been the victim of the reactionary teachings of both old parties which have led to your attempted assassination. The country needs you, and separating myself from past party associations I pledge you my earnest and unqualified support for your second elective term as President of the United States.[7]

Although Dickinson sometimes refused to support candidates nominated by his party in his last years, he still considered himself a true Democrat—a Jeffersonian Democrat. To one who asked him to furnish "some sound Democratic doctrine," he advised the reading of a good biography of Jefferson or Jackson. He made known his admiration for Jefferson by agreeing to serve as vice president for Michigan of the Thomas Jefferson Memorial Association.

Like Jefferson, Dickinson revealed a basic belief in a democracy that would uphold the interests and rights of all men. He had demonstrated this conviction quite dramatically in his long struggle against those who tried to evict the homesteaders from their farms in the Upper Peninsula. In his support of the popular election of senators, in his effort to make railroads pay a fair amount of taxes in Detroit, and in his support of a tariff that would favor the interests of the lower income group, Dickinson was convinced that he was practicing the principles that Jefferson and Jackson had championed years before.

Dickinson, though wealthy himself, had sympathy for the common man, the man who was equal to him but perhaps had not enjoyed an equal chance. He revealed this in a letter written to Secretary of War William Howard Taft in 1905. In this note Dickinson made a strong plea in behalf of George Baker, a deserter from the Army, whose mother had been employed in the Dickinson house. He explained, "My interest and my duty lies in this: That the mother of the man, Mrs. Jennie E. Baker, is now supporting a large family of children including three young sons at school, by the labor of her own hands. This George Baker, her eldest son, had been accustomed to contribute from his pay to the support of his mother and family." Pleading young Baker's cause as fervently as he would plead that of any of his wealthy clients, Dickinson sought to have mercy shown.

78

Dickinson demonstrated the same compassion when he wrote of the pleasure he derived from hearing that his daughter Frances was going to have a Christmas where "little girls who are not poor in anything else than mere money" would have a part. He knew that his daughter would not make little girls who were poor in material things feel inferior. "Clothes and food are all the difference, and clothes and food don't make one person any better than another. My dear daughter knows when she refers to the teaching of the Great and Gentle Teacher of the world that there are no differences like this and that in His view there are no 'poor' souls or 'poor' hearts in the sense that one soul or one heart is more valuable or of more importance than another."

After 1896, although still very active in his legal practice, Dickinson found time for things which his political activities had seemed to limit before that time. His correspondence indicates that he now enjoyed more hours with his wife and two children. Although he did not visit Cleveland often, he corresponded with him until the retired President's death. During these years Dickinson continued to offer advice to the former President on various matters. For example, Cleveland sought Dickinson's counsel regarding an able biographer. Dickinson advised that a man be chosen "who has the 'knack' and dexterity of stating incidents which really make a history or biography interesting." Dickinson's regard for Cleveland compelled him to say that any biographer of Cleveland should not make the biography an "avocation." "He should devote himself to it and be near you for consultation as a portrait painter is near his work to take frequent 'looks' and so get the familiar expression and so on." Dickinson was convinced that a "high class literary man should do it." He suggested Richard W. Gilder or one of Cleveland's Harvard or Princeton friends. In 1910, Gilder published *Grover Cleveland: A Record of Friendship.*

During the years that Cleveland lived, Dickinson remained active. He denied stories that he was ill. In 1906, he wrote Cleveland, "I never was more robust, never weighed so much, never endured hard work more serenely or did so much as now. . . ." His correspondence, his continued interest in his family, his law practice, and his home all indicate that this was true. In 1908, the year Cleveland died, he began to feel the strain of a life that had been filled with so many varied activities. Although a New York newspaper erred when, in April, 1908, it published a report that Dickinson was "at death's door," it is true that Dickinson sharply curtailed his activities after this time.

Although he was able in 1911 to appear in court in his own behalf and defend himself successfully against those who claimed he was incompetent to administer his own property, Dickinson by that time was only a shadow of his former self. Cancer had begun to ravage his body. After 1912, he went into almost complete seclusion and until the end of his life spent much time reading in his large, comfortable library at his home in Trenton, Michigan.

On Monday, October 15, 1917, Dickinson died quietly after uttering the words, "The peace of God that passeth all understanding will soon be mine."[8] On October 17, the day of his funeral, flags flew at half mast on all Post Office buildings throughout the United States. Although he had been inactive for several years, citizens in all stations reflected upon his contributions. President Woodrow Wilson aptly described the sentiments of many when he wired: "I have learned with deep regret of the death of Honorable Don M. Dickinson who in his life illustrated a very high type of American citizenship, who devoted many years to the public service, and who leaves a memory that will be cherished and revered not only by the people of his state, but by the people of his nation."

* * * * * *

After Dickinson died, the *Detroit News* observed that Michigan had produced two Democratic leaders in national politics during the eighty years it had been a state—Lewis Cass and Donald M. Dickinson. No other Michigan leaders "had larger voice in the councils" of the Democratic party. None were "more potent with national administrators." The *News* pointed out that Cass exerted leadership in the years when his party was in control of five Democratic Presidents. On the other hand, Dickinson "came into leadership when the party was beginning to emerge from the shadows of disaster that politics and conditions responsible for the Civil War brought upon it, and when Michigan had become overwhelmingly Republican." The *News* concluded that, because of this, Dickinson "did not have the opportunity to make as great an impression in the history of the Democratic party" as did Cass. Still, "in the administrations of the only Democratic President during his leadership he assuredly wielded as much political power as did Cass."

The evidence indicates that this is true. There seems to be little doubt that especially in matters of patronage Dickinson exercised a great deal of influence. Fellow Michiganians such as George Lothrop, Edwin F. Uhl, and Henry T. Thurber would not have gained their positions without Dickinson. President Cleveland expressed his esteem for Dickinson and implied that his influence was significant when he said, "A few more Dickinsons . . . would save our party." On another occasion he wrote, "I am constantly wondering why there are not within the circle of my life, more Lamonts and Dickinsons." As has been made plain, Cleveland's trust caused him to rely heavily upon Dickinson when making federal appointments. As postmaster general, Dickinson could directly favor certain individuals while withholding his blessing from others.

Within Michigan, Dickinson did much to revitalize his party, to transform it "into a battleground where a few thousand votes tipped the balance." In his time the climax came in the Wolverine State when the Democrats trounced the Republicans in the 1890 elections.

Dickinson was an able politician: this partially accounts for his rise within the Democratic party. The fact that he was a friend of President Cleveland served to enhance his position within the state organization. There were times when this friendship stood him in good stead. For example, after Dickinson had scored an impressive and unexpected victory at the April, 1896 Democratic state convention, he expressed surprise over the anti-administration delegation from Grand Rapids, particularly "after the appointment of a citizen of that district and city to the great post of ambassader to Germany." Although the appointment of Edwin F. Uhl of Grand Rapids to this position apparently had not influenced the Furniture City delegation on this occasion, Dickinson implied that in most cases such an appointment would have won delegates to the administration's side. Some Michigan Democrats knew that Dickinson had the kind of power to effect such an appointment and for this reason were willing to defer to him. For good reason, some called him president for Michigan, while others admitted that without Dickinson the state would not have been favored as it had been by the Cleveland administration. Still others grudgingly conceded that Dickinson's good will was needed to gain any appointments, and therefore it was best to cooperate with Cleveland's lieutenant.

Dickinson was an innovator regarding party organization. However, he, like Cleveland and many other reformers of the late nineteenth century, was basically conservative in his conception of the role of government.[9] He believed in elimination of corruption and thus stressed reform in several of the campaigns that he directed. Cleveland's stand on the tariff was his stand; a high tariff seemingly coddled industry, and in the minds of men like Dickinson equal opportunity should exist for all. The currency was not to be expanded or inflated artificially to meet the demands of a certain segment of the population. Government was to be partial to no one; its role was to prevent injustice, but its function was not to effect positive good. This often resulted in a *laissez faire*, "that government which governs least, governs best" philosophy. This partly accounts for Dickinson's admiration of Thomas Jefferson.

Dickinson's attitude toward the government's role changed in the early years of the twentieth century. One begins to see this change as early as 1904, when he backed Judson Harmon rather than Alton B. Parker for the Democratic presidential nomination. It was even more obvious that Dickinson was becoming convinced that government should play a more positive role when he supported Theodore

Roosevelt and the Bull Moose party in 1912. Roosevelt had proposed a new nationalism which regarded "the executive power as the steward of the public welfare." Dickinson apparently agreed with much of Roosevelt's program, for he stated that Roosevelt had "been the victim of the reactionary teachings of both old parties"; Roosevelt, in Dickinson's mind, was the type of man that the country needed.

NOTES

CHAPTER 1. "HERE MY FATHER FOUGHT . . . HERE WILL I FIGHT"

[1] Jerome Dickinson to Asa C. Dickinson, Dec. 1, 1850, Dickinson Papers, Michigan Historical Commission Archives, hereinafter cited as MHCA. Papers made available through the courtesy of George Wiskemann.

[2] Arthur Pound, *Detroit: Dynamic City* (New York, 1940), pp. 170-183.

[3] *Trial of Charles A. Edmonds* (Lansing, 1872), I, 3-44.

[4] *Michigan Almanac*, 1873 (Detroit, 1873), p. 85.

CHAPTER 2. "REACHING THE TOPMOST ROUND OF THE LADDER"

[1] Harriette M. Dilla, *The Politics of Michigan, 1865-1878* (New York, 1912), p. 171.

[2] John W. Lederle and Rita F. Aid, "Michigan State Party Chairmen: 1882-1956," *Michigan History*, XLI (1957), 258.

[3] *Detroit Free Press*, June 9, 1880. Both the *Free Press* and the *Evening News* contain extensive accounts of the state convention.

[4] Allan Nevins, *Grover Cleveland: A Study in Courage* (New York, 1932), p. 135.

[5] *Detroit News*, Oct. 17, 1917.

CHAPTER 3. "I HAVE NOT LOST A PARTICLE OF MY CONFIDENCE IN YOU"

[1] See the sketch about Dickinson by Arthur Pound in E. D. Babst and L. G. Vander Velde (eds.), *Michigan and the Cleveland Era* (Ann Arbor, 1948), pp. 109-136.

CHAPTER 4. "COMING DOWN THERE"

[1] Dorothy G. Fowler, *The Cabinet Politician: The Postmasters General, 1829-1909* (New York, 1943), p. 206.

[2] Donald M. Dickinson, "Progress and the Post," *North American Review*, CXLIX (1889), 399-412.

CHAPTER 5. "YOU HAVE DONE GLORIOUSLY"

[1] Allan Nevins (ed.), *Letters of Grover Cleveland, 1850-1908* (Boston, 1933), pp. 245-246.

[2] Allan Nevins, *Grover Cleveland: A Study in Courage* (New York, 1932), p. 468.

[3] *Ibid.*, pp. 483-484.

[4] George H. Knoles, *The Presidential Campaign and Election of 1892* (Palo Alto, 1942), pp. 216-220.

[5] Robert McElroy, *Grover Cleveland: The Man and the Statesman* (New York, 1923), I, 332-333.

[6] Nevins, *Grover Cleveland*, p. 487.

[7] Knoles, *The Campaign of 1892*, p. 84.

[8] Nevins, *Grover Cleveland*, p. 497.

CHAPTER 6. "YOU WILL HEAR NO MORE OF DICKINSON"

[1] E. D. Babst and L. G. Vander Velde (eds.), *Michigan and the Cleveland Era* (Ann Arbor, 1948), pp. 249-250.

[2] Allan Nevins, *Grover Cleveland: A Study in Courage* (New York, 1932), pp. 515-516.

[3] *Detroit Evening News*, May 19, 1893.

[4] *Detroit Evening News*, June 29, 1894.

[5] *Detroit Evening News*, Sept. 24, 1894.

[6] Mark D. Hirsch, *William C. Whitney: Modern Warwick* (New York, 1948), p. 487.

[7] Hirsch, *Whitney*, p. 488.

[8] Nevins, *Grover Cleveland*, p. 698.

[9] Horace S. Merrill, *William Freeman Vilas: Doctrinaire Democrat* (Madison, 1954), p. 237.

[10] James A. Barnes, "The Gold-Standard Democrats and the Party Conflict," *Mississippi Valley Historical Review*, XVII (1930), 445-446.

CHAPTER 7. "A MEMORY... CHERISHED AND REVERED... BY THE PEOPLE OF HIS NATION"

[1] John B. Moore, *A Digest of International Law* (Washington, 1906), I, 920.

[2] Robert McElroy, *Grover Cleveland: The Man and the Statesman* (New York, 1923), II, 296.

[3] Elting E. Morison (ed.), *The Letters of Theodore Roosevelt* (Cambridge, 1951), II, 1411-1412.

[4] Allan Nevins, *Grover Cleveland: A Study in Courage* (New York, 1932), pp. 752-753.

[5] McElroy, *Cleveland*, II, 317-318.

[6] Donald M. Dickinson to Jacob M. Dickinson, June 27, 1904, Dickinson Papers, MHCA.

[7] Donald M. Dickinson to T. Roosevelt, Oct. 16, 1912, Dickinson Papers, MHCA.

[8] Interview with Donald M. Dickinson, Jr., July 16, 1968. Mr. Dickinson is the only surviving child of Donald M. Dickinson. He was born in 1890 and now lives in St. Clair Shores, Michigan.

[9] See Ari Hoogenboom, "An Analysis of Civil Service Reformers," *The Historian*, XXIII (1960), 54-78. Also Richard Hofstadter, *The American Political Tradition and the Men Who Made It* (New York, 1948), pp. 162-182; and Horace S. Merrill, *Bourbon Democracy of the Middle West, 1865-1896* (Baton Rouge, 1953).

BIBLIOGRAPHICAL ESSAY

Various manuscript collections proved valuable in writing this book. The Library of Congress has six boxes of Donald M. Dickinson material. This collection is not catalogued, but it is small enough so that it can be examined carefully. The Grover Cleveland Papers, the William C. Whitney Papers, and the Daniel S. Lamont Papers, all located in the Library of Congress, were helpful in describing Dickinson's role in national political affairs. Also useful in determining the part that Dickinson played in the 1892 and 1896 campaigns were a number of letters which he wrote to William F. Vilas of Wisconsin. Photostat copies of these letters along with microfilm copies of some of the Dickinson-Cleveland correspondence can be found in the Michigan Historical Collections at the University of Michigan. The Burton Historical Collection in the Detroit Public Library has a small collection of Dickinson material. A very fascinating series of letters sent by a rabid, anti-Catholic organization to Dickinson at the time of the 1892 Democratic convention is included in this collection.

Newspapers proved beneficial in gathering information, especially about political activity of the day. Two Detroit newspapers, the *Evening News* and the *Free Press*, published daily editions during the time of Dickinson's prominence in Michigan politics. Since Dickinson was from Detroit, most of his activities as a public figure were given detailed coverage. These newspapers, along with others, are available on microfilm at the State of Michigan's library in Lansing.

Of great value to me in describing the Dickinson-Cleveland relationship after 1884 were two biographies of Grover Cleveland. Probably the most helpful was *Grover Cleveland: A Study in Courage* by Allan Nevins (New York, 1932), although the two-volume biography by Robert McElroy, *Grover Cleveland: The Man and the Statesman* (New York, 1923), also did much to illuminate the Cleveland-Dickinson association. Allan Nevins has collected and edited much of the significant Cleveland correspondence and published this under the title *Letters of Grover Cleveland 1850-1908* (Boston, 1933).

Earl D. Babst and Lewis C. Vander Velde have edited *Michigan and the Cleveland Era* (Ann Arbor, 1948), which contains a number of sketches of University of Michigan staff members and alumni who served in the Cleveland administrations, several of whom were associated with Dickinson.

There are several other books about important leaders and developments of the Cleveland-Dickinson era. Some that were useful to me in writing this book include: James A. Barnes, *John G. Carlisle: Financial Statesman* (New York, 1931); Harriette M. Dilla, *The Politics of Michigan, 1865-1878* (New York, 1912); Sidney Fine, *Laissez Faire and the General-Welfare State: A Study of Conflict in American Thought, 1865-1901* (Ann Arbor, 1956); Mark D. Hirsch, *William C. Whitney: Modern Warwick* (New York, 1948); Stanley L. Jones, *The Presidential Election of 1896* (Madison, 1964); Matthew Josephson, *The Politicos, 1865-1896* (New York, 1938); George H. Knoles, *The Presidential Campaign and Election of 1892* (Palo Alto, 1942); Horace S. Merrill, *Bourbon Democracy of the Middle West, 1865-1896* (Baton Rouge, 1953); and by the same author, *Bourbon Leader: Grover Cleveland and the Democratic Party* (Boston, 1957), and *William Freeman Vilas: Doctrinaire Democrat* (Madison, 1954); and George F. Parker, *Recollections of Grover Cleveland* (New York, 1909).